PLAN AND ORGANIZE YOUR *life*

PLAN AND ORGANIZE YOUR *life*

Achieve Your Goals by Creating Intentional Habits and Routines for Success

BEATRICE NAUJALYTE

yellow pear press

Coral Gables

Cover & Layout Design: Carmen Fortunato
Cover Photo: Photographee.eu / Adobe Stock

For permission requests, please contact the publisher at:
Mango Publishing Group
2850 S Douglas Road, 2nd Floor
Coral Gables, FL 33134 USA
info@mango.bz

For special orders, quantity sales, course adoptions and corporate sales, please email the publisher at sales@mango.bz. For trade and wholesale sales, please contact Ingram Publisher Services at customer.service@ingramcontent.com or +1.800.509.4887.

Plan and Organize Your Life: Achieve Your Goals by Creating Intentional Habits and Routines for Success

Library of Congress Cataloging-in-Publication number: 2021941067
ISBN: (print) 978-1-64250-677-8, (ebook) 978-1-64250-678-5
BISAC category code SEL035000, SELF-HELP / Self-Management / Time Management

Printed in the United States of America

For all of the readers and viewers of *The Bliss Bean*.
You guys inspire me more than I inspire you.

TABLE OF CONTENTS

V. HABITS, ROUTINES, & TRACKING 186

FOREWORD

I am honoured to be writing the foreword for this book, and I am so excited for you, the reader, to be taking this huge step toward a more organized and intentional life.

For those of you who don't know me, I'm Cassandra Aarssen. I am the creator of Clutterbug™, an organizing business that helps hundreds of thousands of families all over the world get organized. I am also the host of HGTV's *Hot Mess House* and author of four bestselling organizing books. I'm telling you this because I want you to know that, just ten short years ago, I was a stay-at-home mom drowning in clutter and living paycheck to paycheck; every aspect of my life was a complete disaster. It wasn't until my late thirties that I finally discovered the power of planning, routines, and organization. When I began goal planning, organizing, and implementing easy routines, my entire life was transformed in a very short amount of time. Not only did my home look and function better, but I gained control of my finances, had more time and energy for friends and hobbies, and I was able to build an incredible business, all while being a mom to three children. Imagine if I had started at a younger age!

That is why I am so excited for you to be reading this book at this moment in your life. Beatrice is such an inspiration to so many through her blog and YouTube channel, and the most impressive part for me is that most of her followers are young adults.

The fact that you are reading this book means you already have a head start, and I want you to really let that sink in. In the pages of this book, you will learn life lessons that will impact every single area of your life in a positive way. Taking a dream and turning it into a plan is how magic is made, and this book will walk you through how to do that. I was always a big dreamer, but I didn't know how to take those dreams from wishing and hoping to doing and succeeding. Planning didn't come naturally to me and, honestly, I didn't take the time to learn until my life was completely falling apart. You are giving yourself such a gift by starting right now.

If I had to pinpoint just *one thing* that made the biggest impact on my overall success, it was starting small and simple routines. Structure, discipline, and schedules are NOT my thing. I like to think I'm a free spirit, and I certainly don't want to be forced into any sort of "box." I always thought that having routines would be stifling and strict. I assumed having daily and weekly routines would limit my freedom, when in fact, routines give my life so much *more* freedom. My routines are simple, but they gift me with more time, more energy, more focus, and much more happiness. I am able to achieve HUGE and seemingly impossible goals for myself because my daily routines keep me on track and keep me moving toward that bigger picture.

So congratulations, I really mean that. This book is going to walk you through the easy and simple steps that you need to create that roadmap for your own life. Anything is possible, you just need to keep taking the right steps down your personal road toward success. This book has just given you a huge head start.

—Cassandra Aarssen, author of *The Declutter Challenge* and *Cluttered Mess to Organized Success*

PART I

INTRODUCTION

instead of FINDING time, MAKE time

This is a mantra that has stuck with me for years. Perhaps it's not congruent with Einstein's theories about space-time—I'm a blogger, not a physicist—but it certainly is an inspiring reminder that, with a little bit of effort and careful planning, you can *create* time, almost as if by magic, to do the things you love, spend time with the people you love, and design a life you love.

I'll be honest with you: I haven't always been good at time management. Actually, I used to really, really suck at it, and procrastination was the name of my game. I firmly believed that a few extra minutes of sleep were worth rushing into school past the bell, and I treated "due" dates as "do" dates. In middle school, I would complain about homework taking up my entire evening, without realizing that maybe, just maybe, I would get it done faster if I didn't have my phone glued to my hand to text my friends every two minutes.

So you see, I *felt* like I was working hard... I was stressed out. Check. I had a packed schedule. Check. I was exhausted and caught every single cold that went around the school because my immune system took the brunt of my poor self-care habits. Check.

Let's take stock of where I was at:

- I *wanted* to do well in school, but in reality, I was sinking all of my time into unproductive study habits and investing way too much time and energy into my grades.

- I *wanted* to spend more time with my family, but in reality, I always passed on doing fun things with them because I couldn't possibly imagine fitting them into my weekly schedule.

- I *wanted* to develop my hobbies, but I said yes to absolutely everything and used up all of my energy on an assortment of activities that hardly brought me joy.

I was busy and outwardly successful but frazzled and not all that productive. I decided that I needed to make a change.

In high school, I began following different bloggers who shared tips on an organized life and started experimenting with my own planning and organization methods. I bought cute little agendas to write my weekly tasks in, and even fashioned my own (far less cute) paper planner with scraps of plastic and hole-punched paper. The extent to which these experiments actually improved my productivity is debatable, but I took great pride in my color-coded creations.

The summer before my junior year, however, I decided to take a different approach. Rather than categorizing my tasks by every imaginable attribute and spending hours designing planner layouts, I simply wanted to see where my time was going. Yeah, I knew I was busy, but busy doing *what,* exactly? I downloaded a time-tracking app as an experiment and started tracking every minute of my day. My friends were a little confused when they saw my graphs and charts.

"Wait, how does this app know when you go to the bathroom?" (I entered all of that manually.)

Seeing exactly how I spent my time forced me to get honest with myself regarding my systems and commitments. Once I identified where I was sinking too much of my time and where I needed to invest more of it, I dove headfirst into the world of planning, productivity, and organization. I combed through articles and self-help books, deploying further experiments to test the different methods I learned about. Everything from the Pomodoro technique and Eisenhower matrices to time blocking and "eating the frog" (we'll get to that later).

As I picked my favorite techniques and began to implement them, every area of my life started to improve. I was able to get things done faster, maintain good grades with far less effort, relax and recharge with family and friends... and start *The Bliss Bean* in 2017.

design a life
you LOVE.

The Bliss Bean

The Story of *The Bliss Bean*

With this new passion for personal development, I suddenly started looking at every area of my life through a lens of improvement and optimization. I wanted to understand not only how to be more "productive," but more specifically, how to work more efficiently on the *right* things in order to design a life I loved.

Of course, I won't claim that my entire life changed the moment I cracked open a self-improvement book and I suddenly had it "all figured out." Just like any high school student, I was still lacking sleep and balancing an uncomfortable number of plates. However, I felt on top of things in a way I'd never felt before, and I was genuinely excited to keep learning more. That difference was immeasurable.

In July 2017, I finally decided to start the blog I had always dreamed of. I had dabbled in craft blogs as a kid, but now I wanted to share what I was learning about. I started to carve out time during evenings and weekends to create content about personal development, productivity, and mindfulness. It was almost like an online journal; it documented my growth and evolved with my interests, and the audience I grew became something like a family. It only made sense that they would be a part of this book.

Meet *The Bliss Bean* readers and viewers who contributed their personal planning and organization tips to every section of this book. Look out for blurbs from them!

> **ALICE PREECE** is a final year university student in Sheffield, England. She studies journalism and loves nothing more than meticulously planning out her life each week (except for maybe binging BTS YouTube videos...).

ANA MORA is a literature student in Chile. She uses her bullet journal to plan out her schoolwork, reading assignments, and events to make sure everything is finished before the due date.

ANTONIA SARAFOVA is from Bulgaria and is currently studying creative business at BUAS in The Netherlands while growing her brand as a micro-influencer.

CARLOTTA URBAN is a high school student from Germany who uses her planning systems to manage schoolwork and many creative hobbies like a poetry Instagram account and theater classes.

CAROLINE THEUERKAUF is a junior triple majoring in political science, international and comparative studies, and German at a university in the US. She uses a combination of digital and paper planning systems to organize her schoolwork, extracurriculars, and volunteer work.

CRISTINA BARRANCOS lives in Portugal and teaches Portuguese to English-speaking students. She uses a variety of paper and digital tools to book lessons, schedule her day, and manage tasks.

JOY SHIM is a PhD candidate studying philosophy in the United States. Although she loves pens and paper, she has seen the digital light and can never go back.

KATIE RENNICK is a listing specialist for a local property management company in Florida. She's an iPad fanatic and uses GoodNotes and Pinterest to design the aesthetic of her work and life.

KEERTHI is a gap year student in India who spent her gap year waking up early to self-study topics like particle physics, digital art, and quantum computing. She believes productivity is more about learning and having fun than getting things done.

KIMBERLY HOHMEYER is an eleventh grade student in Germany. She uses her bullet journal to plan out her schoolwork and personal to-dos for each day.

KYLA BERTRAND is a culinary arts management student in London. She uses a paper planner to list her top three priorities each day.

MARIAH is a freshman in college from Montana, USA, studying molecular and cellular biology. She loves to sing, dance, and make schedules to her heart's content.

MAWADDA TARIG is an artist and a German language teacher from Sudan studying electrical engineering. She enjoys art and uses a bullet journal, Notion, and a DIY scheduling board for her planning.

MAX GONZÁLEZ GARCÍA is finishing a psychology degree in Spain and plans on going to music school afterwards. He uses a mix of paper and digital tools to juggle tasks like music practice and homework.

SAHAANAA HARIHARAN is an Indian eleventh grade student who likes to go with the flow when it comes to her planning systems, whether that means making to-do lists on sticky notes or tracking habits in Notion.

SANDRA PATRICIA RUELAS LISBOA is a college freshman studying marketing in Puerto Rico and a list-maker since the age of seven. She loves art and posts content to her blog and YouTube channel.

SHIVANI SHAH is a dental student studying in the UK. She curates an intentional life so she can focus more time on the essential. Currently, that consists of building good habits and sharing meaningful content on her YouTube channel *Dental Shiv*.

SHRUTI BASKAR is a textile design student from India and has been using the bullet journal for three to four years. She uses a combination of Notion and bullet journaling to manage her academic goals and personal habits.

TRIVYA LUTHRA is a high school freshman in India and uses a bullet journal to organize her life, including endless school assignments and interests like language learning.

ZUZANNA CZOPIK is a Polish communications and media student at a British university. She prefers planning on paper, using mind maps and a bullet journal to break down her academic and social media management side hustle projects into bite-sized tasks.

Today, I'm grateful for every part of my personal development journey. If I had not started in a place of procrastination and constant stress, I wouldn't have looked for something better and stumbled upon this passion of mine. I've gotten the grades I wanted, started my own photography business, gotten into my dream college, and grown *The Bliss Bean* into my full-time dream job, garnering over ten million views on YouTube and now writing the book you hold in your hands!

Why Plan?

I know, I know, all of this planning and organization can seem like way too much work for some faint future benefits. I promise you, though, it is worth it. Here are a few reasons why:

1. *It feels really good to get things done.* You know that feeling when you finish a big project? When you get some annoying to-do off your shoulders? Or when you finish a long day of crossing off important tasks? By optimizing the way you work, you'll experience that feeling of accomplishment much more often (hopefully, every single day!)

2. *You'll feel more confident.* Setting goals and putting in consistent work toward them over the long run builds your trust in yourself and creates a deep-seated sense of confidence. You'll realize that you're capable of so much more than you thought.

3. *You'll have more free time.* The goal of these planning techniques is not to simply fit more work into the day, but rather to spend more time on what matters most. You'll be able to schedule time with friends and family, block out time for relaxation, and develop your side hustles and passion projects.

4. *Your "someday" will become a reality.* While you may be getting by without any sort of planning and organization system and completing your most urgent tasks right at the buzzer without missing any deadlines, chances are, you have a list in your head of things you would like to do "someday" that your frantic, last-minute schedule leaves no time for. Imagine if you could actually achieve those bucket list goals!

5. *You'll understand yourself better.* Having a system for capturing, taking action on, and reviewing your thoughts, dreams, and ideas is a big step toward developing a healthy relationship with yourself.

Make a bucket list of those "someday" things that you'll be able to do once you have a good planning and organization system in place.

Be able to cook better meals

To have a nice home

To Be able to garden

Start a business

Read more

Feel better - prolong my life

More energy

Travel more

Better with my money

closer to Family

Write a Book (maybe)

settle down - roots

organize my stuff

Where to Start?

Before we dive into designing the perfect planning and organization system for you, let's start with doing an audit of your current systems! Aspiring "organizers" often spread themselves out among a jumble of different tools that catch their eye, so let's assess where all of your to-dos, notes, and ideas currently live.

Make a list of all of the tools you currently use to organize/plan your life: mobile apps, web apps, notebooks, bullet journals, paper planners and calendars, digital calendars, Post-it notes, random napkins, the back of your hand, anything! As you design your new planning and organization system, make sure you transfer over any important information.

I have so many calendars and planners and none are perfect. I have lots of organizational books

Our goal throughout this process is to simplify. That doesn't mean that you need to find the one magical tool that will solve everything (if you've been able to find that, please share your secret with me). What it does mean, however, is that you will achieve a state of organized bliss through the *minimum* number of different tools that YOU need. I've compiled a list of resources, including budgeting spreadsheets and time tracking categories (both of which we'll get into a bit later), to help you achieve your personal organization goals. You can find these examples and more at theblissbean.com/bookresources.

Just like an organized home requires that every item has a designated place, an organized life requires that every piece of information has its place as well. With an organized system, you always know exactly where your notes, appointments, plans, and ideas are. The less you're keeping track of and juggling in your mind, the more room there is to achieve clarity and for true creativity to flow.

in an ORGANIZED system, every piece of INFORMATION has a designated place.

The Four Pillars of Planning and Organization that We'll Cover in This Book:

✣ *Planning*: We will first put into place a system to track all of your to-dos in life and learn how to implement regular yearly, monthly, weekly, and daily planning routines to ensure that nothing slips through the cracks..

✣ *Organization*: Then, we'll move on to organizing your tools and thoughts (your physical workspace, your digital files, your phone, etc.) and your system for capturing ideas and notes.

✣ *Productivity*: No *Bliss Bean* book would be complete without a discussion of productivity techniques. Don't worry, you don't have to implement them all! We'll talk about tried-and-tested techniques that you can pick and choose to design your own "productivity toolbox."

✣ *Habits and Routines*: Finally, we'll close out the book by designing some habits and routines to keep you moving forward and growing. After all, your dream life is created not in one sitting, but through small daily actions.

let's begin!

PART II

PLANNING

Chapter 1

Assembling Your Planning Toolbox

If you're searching this book for advice because you're "just not good at planning," stop right there. Planning is just like creativity (which many people also claim to be "not good" at). While some are born with a predisposition for organizing, it is a skill and muscle that anyone can build through simple practice. The habits and mindsets of planning proactively may not come naturally to you now, but trust that through implementing these techniques and witnessing firsthand how much more intentional and fulfilling your life can be, you can become "one of those planner people" too.

If you currently have no planning system to speak of, the first thing you'll need to do is build the daily habit of checking in with your plans. Try to pair it with one of your existing habits, so that an action that is already automatic to you triggers the new one you are trying to develop. Do you drink coffee at the kitchen table every morning? Leave your planner there and look over your plan for the day as you caffeinate. Do you spend some time scrolling your phone before you go to sleep? Leave your planner on the bedside table and take a moment to review the day *before* you pick up your phone. Just a few minutes of focus each day is all you need.

Calendars

Before we get into the big picture of turning your dreams into daily actions, let's look at how you manage the day-to-day of your busy life. A calendar is an essential tool to keep track of your commitments, remember important dates, and understand how you're using your time. You'll first need to choose whether a digital calendar or an analog one suits you best:

Digital	Paper
+ It syncs across all of your devices. + It can notify you of upcoming events automatically. + It allows for easy shuffling and rearranging of your schedule. + It has room for lots of extra event information such as address, invitees, web links, notes, etc. + It can repeat events automatically, so you never have to think about rescheduling.	+ Physically writing down your commitments can help you remember them better. + A paper calendar never needs to be recharged. + It can be highly visible if displayed on your desk or on the wall.
- A calendar that lives in the "cloud" can be easy to forget about (out of sight, out of mind...). - You can't create an event if you don't have your phone or computer with you. - There are possible privacy concerns.	- It can be misplaced, thus losing all of your important information. - You may not have it with you when you need to check it to schedule an event. - It can get messy if you need to edit it often. - It's harder to visualize how much of your day an event actually takes up without a timeline view. - It can't be synced with other people's calendars.

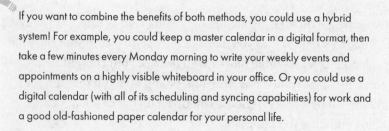

If you want to combine the benefits of both methods, you could use a hybrid system! For example, you could keep a master calendar in a digital format, then take a few minutes every Monday morning to write your weekly events and appointments on a highly visible whiteboard in your office. Or you could use a digital calendar (with all of its scheduling and syncing capabilities) for work and a good old-fashioned paper calendar for your personal life.

Tools for Calendars

- **iCal:** *Free.* It comes pre-installed on Apple devices, so if you already have an iPhone and/or Mac, picking something that's part of the digital ecosystem you already use makes things easier. On the other hand, if you use Android or Windows devices, you're out of luck. iCal allows you to color-code events, add additional information, set alerts and repeating schedules, and add invitees via email. You can sync it with Google Calendar, but collaborating across different platforms can get a little tricky, so you might want to take into account what your coworkers and family use if you need to share events with them.

- **Google Calendar:** *Free.* A popular calendar that works well with the Google ecosystem (Gmail, Google Drive, Google Meet, etc.) and is available on pretty much any digital device you might use. As with most calendar tools, you can create multiple calendars, share them with other people, customize alerts, schedule repeating events, add attachments, invite guests, etc.

Personally, I prefer the design of iCal but needed some of the collaborative features of Google Calendar, so I signed into my Google account through iCal to sync the two!

- **Microsoft Outlook:** *Free. Upgraded plans available.* This calendar tool integrates with the Microsoft Office apps (like Outlook email) and is often used by large organizations.

- **Fantastical:** *Paid.* This app is practically a cult favorite. It offers tons of features to make scheduling quick, like natural language entry (you can simply type in "Dentist appointment 10/13 10am alert 45 minutes" to create an event) and various views to visualize your schedule in different ways.

- **Notion:** *Free. Upgraded plans available.* The productivity tool has a calendar view to visualize items in a database based on the dates attached to them. This might be helpful if you already use Notion, but it's not built to be an all-purpose calendar tool. Scheduling repeating events is currently not possible, and it doesn't integrate well with other calendars, emails, or scheduling tools like Calendly.

There are probably more calendar tools out there than you could ever try! Keep in mind that you don't need *all* the fancy bells and whistles. Pick what gets the job done for you.

ZUZANNA, a communication and media university student in England, usually prefers using paper tools, like her bullet journal, for planning, but makes an exception for digital calendars. Rather than a list of events, she prefers a timeline view with blocked out appointments to visualize how much free time she actually has.

As your life changes, so will the tools you use. ALICE used to "live and die" by her Apple Calendar because it synced easily across her Apple Watch, iPhone, and Mac and made it easy to add events on the go. However, while working and studying from home during the pandemic lockdown, she switched to a simpler paper calendar to plan out appointments, lectures, meetings, and self-care activities like calling friends or going for walks.

How to Organize Your Calendar

Separating your events based on category can help you stay organized with a busy schedule. If you use a digital calendar, you can create separate calendars that you can then hide individually from view or share with relevant people. With a paper calendar, you might keep a separate calendar in your kitchen for personal events and one at your office for work appointments or you may use different colors of pens and highlighters to color-code events on the same calendar.

As an example, the categories I personally have for my calendar are: *personal, blog/work, exercise classes,* and *birthdays.*

Separating calendars *might* make it easier for you to organize different areas of your life. However, ALICE prefers to plan her lectures and meetings all together in one calendar because when it's separated, she warns, "You can accidentally hide a calendar and forget that something is happening."

If you're someone who needs to schedule a lot of meetings with other people, follow these tips for efficient scheduling (and fewer back-and-forth email chains!)

* Share your entire work calendar with a loved one or colleague with whom you work closely. They'll be able to see your schedule and plan around it without needing to ask you.

* Use a tool like Calendly to make it easy for others to book slots on your calendar. Calendly syncs with your personal calendars and has oodles of features like automatic reminder emails, daily limits on the number of meetings, and the ability to schedule meetings with multiple people at the same time. I use this all the time whenever I need to schedule a podcast interview or a check-in call!

* Use a tool like Doodle to coordinate schedules with a group of people, whether for a team meeting or a movie night with friends. Anyone who's invited to the poll can select the times that work for them.

* Eliminate the need for back-and-forth emails by investing a bit of time up front to write a good email that achieves the end goal. Cal Newport calls this "process-centric" email in his book, *Deep Work*. For example, if someone wants to schedule a meeting with you, do the work up front to get as many of the details sorted out right away as you can. Here's an example email:

I would love to look over your graphic design portfolio with you! Please send me what you have so far and your updated LinkedIn page, and I'll put together some feedback. I'm available Tuesday from 3:30–4:30 p.m., Wednesday from 10:00–11:00 a.m., and Friday at 12:00–1:00 p.m. If any of those times work for you, let me know and we'll consider the meeting set! If none of those times work for you, you can contact me at [phone number] any time after 5:00 p.m. and we can find a different time. I'll send you a Zoom invite!

CRISTINA teaches Portuguese to English speakers and uses Calendly to book lessons with students which then show up on her Google Calendar. To make sure she has time off to recharge and do her other work, she has set up restrictions on Calendly so that lessons cannot be booked on Thursdays or Sundays.

Later, we'll talk more about how to use your calendar for time blocking and long-term goal planning, but let's pause here for the moment!

If you're currently scattered between calendar tools:

1. Pick your favorite tool(s) to transfer all of your commitments into.

2. Choose categories for your events if it helps to keep things separate (e.g., work, personal, meetings, school, holidays, family, exercise, etc.).

3. Share relevant calendars with anyone who might need access to them.

4. Schedule repeating events for those things that happen on a regular basis.

5. Make sure (if you're using a digital tool) that you have access to this calendar on all of your devices.

Task Management

Not everything goes on your calendar! There are also those seemingly endless lists of "to-dos" that we need to take care of at an unspecified time. We'll talk later about how to minimize your to-dos and break your goals down into tiny steps, but for the time being, let's talk about different ways to track these action items.

Digital	Paper
+ You can sync your tasks across devices. + You can schedule repeating tasks (e.g., weekly chores or a monthly report). + You can add extra information to tasks, like files, links, collaborators, due dates, reminders, priority level, etc.	+ It keeps things simple (extra information can become distracting clutter!). + It allows total freedom to draw, diagram, and sketch however you see fit. + It can be used in environments where electronic devices are not allowed (for example, during class). + It can be a more tangible and focused experience than punching keys and staring at a screen.
- Digital devices can be a distraction when you need to focus on deep work. - It can be easy to forget about your tasks when they live somewhere in the "cloud."	- It can be misplaced—you would lose some very important information! - It gets messy when you need to erase, rewrite, and reschedule a lot.

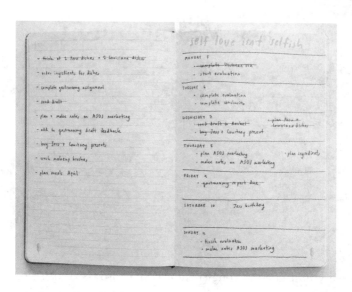

This is a recreation of Kyla's paper diary in which she lists her top three priorities for the day. She keeps it open on her desk so that it's always in view. "Even if you're just passing through your room, it's a good reminder of what you need to get done."

Different Planning Tools

❖ *Store-bought planners*: Premade paper planners usually contain monthly calendars and templates for your daily planning and scheduling. These require little setup on your part, come in various designs, and you can look for a format that includes the features you're looking for.

❖ *Specialty planners*: These are premade paper planners that offer more guidance, like templates for weekly and monthly reviews, goal planning, and journaling. They often have loyal users and strong communities behind them that can give you advice and support (e.g., *Passion Planner, Panda Planner,* Erin Condren *LifePlanner, Happiness Planner*).

❖ *Bullet journals*: This is a DIY system designed by Ryder Carroll that combines your calendar, tasks, and journaling into a standardized system that allows lots of room for customization. While it's often done in creative and beautiful ways, the basic system requires nothing more than a notebook and a pen.

- *Comprehensive task management tools*: These are digital apps that help you to manage complicated projects and tasks. Any feature you are looking for, like assigning tasks to other people and attaching due dates, labels, contexts, etc. can probably be found. Keep in mind that not everyone needs all of these features! However, if you're managing a lot of projects and little tasks simultaneously, a comprehensive program can help you keep track of it all (e.g., Things 3, Omnifocus, Todoist).

- *Simple digital tools*: If you want the convenience of digital without all of the bells and whistles, a simple to do list or checklist app might do the trick. Google users can try Google Keep, Apple Notes is a solid option for iOS, and there are plenty of other apps out there that promise minimal features, like TeuxDeux and MinimaList.

A big draw of paper planning is that it's totally analog. There are no distracting bells and whistles, no pinging notifications to flood your brain with information. If you prefer to plan digitally, give yourself that same opportunity to shut off all distractions. Close unnecessary tabs on your computer, turn off notifications, and keep your screen nice and minimal.

Just like with your calendar, you don't have to go all in on one system. For example, you can use a powerful digital task manager to hold all of your tasks, and then write your daily tasks on a piece of paper to minimize distractions and overwhelm. At the end of the day, you can refer back to the task manager to update what you got done and plan the next day's to-do list. There's a lot of power in analog simplicity! In fact, there was even a popular Kickstarter campaign that raised $450,000 for a wooden stand that holds a paper card with your daily to-dos.

Once in a while, a trendy tool surfaces on YouTube and it seems like every last person on the internet throws away their previous systems to hop on the bandwagon. Remember: just because there's lots of chatter online about a tool doesn't necessarily mean it'll be a good fit for you! Feel free to give it a try, but if it doesn't work for your lifestyle, that's OK!

Personally, I use a simple, daily list-based task manager called TeuxDeux. I've been using this tool since I switched from paper to digital, have tried a few different tools since, but always end up returning to this one. It just matches how my brain works. I like to brain dump my tasks on paper first because the tactile experience of writing gets my brain thinking, and then I transfer tasks into my computer so that I can schedule and manage them easily.

To Summarize...

* Already always at your computer or use your phone a lot? → A to-do list app.

* More simplicity? → A simple notes or checklist app or a bare-bones tool like TeuxDeux.

* Love notebooks and paper and getting creative? → Bullet journaling.

* Need more structure? → Premade planner.

* Even more structure? → Specialty planners like the Passion Planner for time blocking or the Panda planner for priorities and goals.

Experiment! Even though you may have used a system for a while, if something feels off, and especially if your life situation and responsibilities have changed, it might be worth giving something else a test drive. Give yourself a week or two to try out a new tool and decide whether you'd like to continue using it. If it's a match, congrats! If not, you'll learn something from the experiment. You might realize your old system was working just fine or be better informed to try something new.

When **TRIVYA** decided to take a break from her digital planning and try bullet journaling, she felt a bit overwhelmed by the artistry of the setups she saw on YouTube. She reminded herself that she didn't need to replicate the exact layouts that others used; she could customize the system and "create her own recipe."

Project Management

Some undertakings will require more than just a to-do list. Let's start by defining the difference between a project and a task.

A *project* is a super complicated task. It's not something you just put on your to-do list because it can span a week or even years, contain many sub-tasks, and even involve other people. Let's say, for example, you are working with a team to produce a video. Together, you need to create a plan that contains many different types of tasks. You might have to assign certain responsibilities to specific people, update each other on the status of each task, create a timeline and meet deadlines, or keep to a project budget. It's a lot to manage!

An individual *task* of that project might be to go to the camera store to pick up a camera, or to create an online survey to gather feedback on a draft of the video.

You don't necessarily need to work with a team to find a project management tool helpful. I used Trello to plan out my content before I had anyone helping me with *The Bliss Bean* because I could keep track of separate checklists and due dates for each project. If you're a student, you might use a project management tool to plan out how you'll tackle a big research paper, and then add individual tasks like "Go to the library to print all articles" and "Write the conclusion" to your to-do list.

You also don't need to use a fancy project management app! I often plan out projects by opening up a document and just typing out all of my ideas, steps, and deadlines. Basically, the system you use should provide you with a big-picture overview of the various aspects of a specific project, and from there, you'll be able to pull individual action items to add to your to-do list.

Project Management Tools

❖ **Trello:** *Free. Upgraded plans available.* This collaborative tool is based on the Kanban method, meaning "visual signal" in Japanese. A Kanban board contains cards that are moved between columns to indicate what stage of progress each task is at. Imagine putting sticky notes on a whiteboard to track different parts of a project. Trello is basically that, but digital. It's available for web, mobile, and desktop.

❖ **Notion:** *Free. Upgraded plans available.* The increasingly more popular productivity tool is often referred to as "a set of LEGOs." You start with a blank slate, and you can build practically anything you want. You can create pages using a variety of blocks, including text, images, toggle lists, tables, file attachments, and embeds. Tables contain a variety of data types like links, numbers, emails, checkboxes, tags, formulas, and files, and can be viewed in different formats like a table, Kanban board, list, timeline, gallery, and calendar. Filters can be set up so that, for example, your table of "books to read" shows books that you added in the year 2019 with the category label "personal finance." There's an iOS and Android app, a desktop app, and a web version.

❖ **Asana:** *Free. Upgraded plans available.* Asana is similar to Trello, but where Trello focuses heavily on the Kanban view, Asana provides other ways to view your projects and tasks, such as list, board, timeline, calendar, and workload.

These are just a "starter pack" of the plethora of project management tools. Your workplace might already have a preferred tool that they work within, and sometimes, just a good ol' Google Doc or Word document does the trick.

MAWADDA uses Notion to organize the German lessons she teaches. In a detailed page for each lecture, she writes down: What did the students do last lecture? What difficulties did they have with their homework? What do they need to accomplish during this lecture? In her Notion setup, she has also created trackers for each student's progress, checking off attendance, correcting homework, etc. With Notion, everything related to her lessons lives in one organized place! *Gut gemacht!*

A "Catch-all"

Throughout the day, you'll come upon countless bits of important information. At any moment, whether you're waiting for the train or washing your face, random ideas, both good and bad, might pop into your head. Since the goal in developing a planning and organization system is to find a place for everything that's in your mind, a "catch-all" tool serves as a big net to capture everything until you have time to sort it into its proper place.

You might choose to use:

- ❖ a piece of paper or Post-it note on your desk
- ❖ the notes app on your phone
- ❖ the voice memos app
- ❖ a small notebook you carry with you

Pick a set time to process the items on this list before it overflows. You might sit down at the end of the workday or during your evening routine to look through every item and organize it where it belongs, create a task from it, or even just delete it!

- History report due date moved to Friday → Update "school" calendar, move draft editing to Thursday.

- Organize a board game night with friends? → Add to-do: create group chat and Doodle poll to organize board game night.

- Warren talked about wanting to try a spiralizer for zucchini → Add to gift ideas list under "Warren."

- Need to mention my new course on Twitter → Schedule tweets on content calendar.

- Rain tomorrow morning → Set a reminder to bring an umbrella with me.

- BTS concert tickets come out on July 10th → Put on calendar and block off time to buy tickets.

What's Your Keystone?

Here's a new vocab term you can add to your flashcards. You have been making flashcards, right?

A "keystone" is a term from the productivity blog *Ultraworking* to describe something that you look at consistently that tells you what you should be doing. For example, you might have a bullet journal and a habit tracking app, and the very best of intentions to use them consistently, but if your bullet journal remains stashed away at the bottom of a drawer and your habit tracking app hasn't been opened in weeks, those tools are not providing you with much value.

That's why you need a keystone—something you check habitually. According to *Ultraworking*, "A lot of people already have a keystone—either a particular online app, smartphone app, a work journal, putting all your obligations onto the calendar and scheduling them, using a desktop app like Omnifocus, or even a notebook where a person writes their priorities every night and checks them off the next day."

So if you use the Reminders app on your phone consistently, it could be the keystone that reminds you to *also* plan out your day in your bullet journal when you wake up and to check your habit tracker twice a day. If you have a little whiteboard in your office that you see every day, write yourself a note to check the goals in your planner when you arrive at your desk each morning.

If you don't yet have anything that you check on a consistent basis, it will take some time to build that habit, but it'll form a steady foundation that you'll be able to use even if your planning systems change in the future. So go ahead and pick a keystone and do everything in your power to remind yourself to check it—leave Post-it notes on your laptop, change your phone wallpaper, send yourself notifications, and ask your accountability buddy to pester you about it.

A free-flowing approach to planning systems

Rowena Tsai shares self-care tips, productivity techniques, and plenty of planning content on her YouTube channel. I asked her if there are any aspects of her planning system that have remained constant, even when others change. First, she says, "I always have some sort of to-do list, but the actual form of it changes over time." Sometimes, it's a bullet journal. Other times, it's a Post-it Kanban board on the wall. Lately, she's been making checklists in Apple Notes.

Her second essential? Google Calendar for keeping track of all of her appointments and events. "Because I'm so free-flowing with my systems, I need something in place to make sure that I'm communicating properly and I show up on time with the external world."

Rather than developing a rigid system for how she manages her work, she's developed a system of *thought* by cultivating the idea that it's *OK* if her systems change because different seasons of life demand different tools. However, having a consistent keystone at the center of your system helps. All the other techniques that you bring into and out of your life can be considered a part of your "productivity toolbox."

"When specific times of life repeat themselves, whether it be stress, certain demands or projects, things like that," Rowena explains, you can go back to your toolbox to find the technique that served you well in the past.

Chapter 2

Clarifying Your Life Vision

Vision Board

Now that we've picked our tools, let's start making things happen!

Planning should start from the big picture and then zoom into the details. You should get clear on your long-term goals and life vision before you decide how you can use each day to get you closer to that. If you reverse this process, you'll end up bogged down in the minutiae of daily life and never make any meaningful progress toward what really matters most to you. It'd be like trying to pick the perfect painting to hang up in the bedroom of a house before you've even built the frame. You need a foundation before you focus on the details.

To start, we'll zoom out to the largest possible scale. A life vision board! Collecting images and words that inspire you is a great way to start thinking about what you want in life without dwelling on the mechanics of how to actually make that happen.

If you're a practical, logical, no-nonsense kind of person and vision boarding sounds terribly cheesy to you, I totally get it. We won't delve too far into the "woo-woo" in this book, so don't worry about "raising your vibration" to "manifest" what you put on your vision board. I simply encourage you to grab a pair of scissors and some magazines, suspend your judgment for a few minutes, and allow yourself to imagine and play, the way we all did when we were little kids. What do you get excited about when you let go of worrying about the day-to-day stuff that limits your dreams?

Your vision board can include images, words, colors, and quotes that inspire you in any way. If a traditional paper collage doesn't float your boat, you could use a digital tool, like Photoshop, Canva, or Pinterest. You could even get super creative and go the multimedia route and clips to create a video.

Think about different areas of your dream life as you search for elements to include on your board:

- *Environment*: What does your dream home look like? Where do you live? What sorts of places do you spend your time at?

- *Work*: What are you doing for work? What does your workspace look like? How much do you earn? What accolades have you received?

- *Relationships*: What relationships are you developing? How do you spend time with loved ones?

- *Finances*: How much do you have in savings? What are you able to do with money?

- *Health*: How do you feel—physically, mentally, and emotionally—on a daily basis? What healthy habits do you have?

- *Learning*: What languages do you speak? What skills have you developed? Random topics you want to become an expert on?

- *Creativity*: What art do you contribute to the world? Have you written a book, released an album, displayed your paintings in a gallery?

- *Spirituality*: What is your spiritual practice?

- *Fun*: What travel or adventure experiences have you had? How do you spend your free time?

Make it a fun process! Block out an appointment with yourself o[...]
put some nice music on, brew a cup of tea, and take your time. T[...]
display it somewhere in your space!

Sharing your vision board with loved ones or posting it online can [...]
you'd prefer to keep it to yourself, that's fine, too! Remember: this vi.... board is
for you, so don't feel that you need to explain it to anyone but yourself.

Either way, make sure to display it somewhere *you* can see it often.
I printed out square photos and arranged them on a wire grid in my
room that I can look at throughout the day, and I made a collage to use
as my desktop wallpaper. You can also use your vision board as your
phone wallpaper, stick it in your paper planner or journal, or have
mini vision boards hanging in your office, locker, etc.

A Day in Your Dream Life

On the following page, I want you to really stretch your imagination. Look at
your vision board and transport yourself into that life. It's morning, you wake
up, you open your eyes, and you roll out of bed. Fill out the timeline as you
take yourself through the full day, from start to finish. What do you see, hear,
and experience?

5:00	
6:00	
7:00	wake up / shower / get dressed
8:00	work
9:00	
10:00	
11:00	
12:00	lunch- work out
1:00	work
2:00	
3:00	
4:00	430 end day
5:00	start dinner
6:00	Eat & clean up
7:00	watch TV / read / do journal
8:00	830- get ready for bed
9:00	skin / team
10:00	9pm in bed- watch TV
11:00	

There is so much joy in the journey. You can appreciate where you are at now, savor the process, and look forward to your dream life all at the same time.

Searching for Your Personal Polaris

How Do You Want to Feel?

Amy Giddon, the founder and CEO of mindfulness app Daily Haloha, recounts an exercise in which an executive coach asked everyone in the room to write down a personal goal. Among the responses were some ambitious targets like being the director of marketing in six months, quitting a job and starting a farming community, or working less and being at home with their kids more. Next, the participants were asked to write about how they imagined they would feel once they achieved that goal. Accomplished? Balanced? At ease? Here's the plot twist—the executive coach then explained to the group that their *real* goal was their answer to the second question. Deep down, your goal is to *feel* a certain way. Buying some acreage to start a farming community and grow some carrots is just one way to get there.

Isn't this such a freeing way to think about your goals? If you reframe your goal as a *feeling*, then you can find any number of alternative paths to that same destination. If one business idea doesn't work out, perhaps another venture might grant you the same freedom and entrepreneurial thrill that you're chasing. If you can't find a group of like-minded friends in your surroundings, maybe you can join an online group to find that same feeling of support and connectedness that you're looking for. If your initial path turns out to be a dead end, just find a new one and keep marching in the direction of your North Star.

What Is Your North Star?

Having a "North Star" to guide you can keep your focus on the big picture and your perspective open to the range of options that are out there. If you were dropped onto a little sailboat in the middle of an ocean, and all you could see was blue, blue, blue stretching all the way to the horizon, how would you possibly choose a destination? This is what life can feel like at a big crossroads—when graduating high school or college, making a huge career change, or getting through a challenging period of your life, for example.

Instead of having a very specific destination in mind, you can simply orient yourself in a general direction, your North Star: basically, a personal mission statement where you answer, in the broadest sense, what is it that you want to accomplish? What impact do you want to have on the world? How do you want to *feel*?

You can always change your North Star. You can reinvent yourself many times over in your lifetime, but for the time being, you can start by paddling in a direction that feels right to you.

Be like Sherlock and Use Process of Elimination

For the time being, your North Star might be simply to try new things and test hypotheses about what you'd like to do in the long term. After all, who has ever discovered their passion by sitting around and thinking about it? Usually, a passion, a purpose, a life's calling, whatever you want to call it, stems from a series of experiences that might be partially or completely serendipitous. Each experience that you take on is like a small experiment that either confirms or eliminates options. If it doesn't click with you, it's not a "failure." It's just another critical piece of information in the puzzle that is life.

When I was in middle and high school, I loved all things creative. I designed the school yearbook, made the class graduation video, edited the school newspaper, yadda yadda yadda… Logically, I thought it'd be cool to work for some sort of a publication. I could be a creative director at a book publishing company, I thought. Or work at a fashion magazine, à la *The Devil Wears Prada* (minus Meryl Streep yelling at me). I worked on this list in my head, adding job ideas when I stumbled upon someone doing something cool out in the real world and crossing others off when my experiments yielded less than satisfactory results. For example, the day our newspaper club toured the offices of a local daily newspaper, I took one look around the atmosphere and I knew I didn't want to work for a local newspaper... Noted!

What Are Your Absolute Non-Negotiables?

Sometimes, options are eliminated by a gut feeling stemming from a school field trip. Other times, they are eliminated very methodically by laying out personal preferences and non-negotiables. For example, if you are searching for your next job, Amy recommends starting with calculating your cost of living. Financially, how much do you *need* to earn in order to support yourself? Beyond that, what other values and preferences do you need to take into consideration? There are certain things, like a longer commute, that you might be willing to deal with, but if you care deeply about the environment, you might not be able to justify working in the coal mining industry. If you are extremely introverted and work best alone, having a lot of people around you might be an instant disqualifier.

Consider Your Entire "Life Portfolio"

A common mental trap is looking for that *one* perfect job that will satisfy your North Star and check every single box. "Jobs aren't your only opportunity to do things!" Amy points out. If your North Star is to work toward protecting the environment by fighting the climate crisis, but you can't find a career that matches those goals, can you get your job done in forty hours per week and do your environmental work outside of that? Or let's say you find a perfect job working for a nonprofit group, but it doesn't pay enough; perhaps it leaves enough time to tutor on the weekends? In a nutshell, Amy recommends that you ask yourself this question: "Does the job **present** or **prevent** other opportunities in life that check other boxes?"

Ikigai, Hedgehog, and Other Names for Your North Star

There are many terms out there to describe finding that thing in life that guides your journey. For example, you may have heard of ikigai, a Japanese concept that translates as "a reason for being." There's also James C. Collins's "Hedgehog Concept," which suggests that in order to find their one sweet spot, companies need to find the intersection of what they're passionate about, what they're best in the world at, and what drives their economic engine. (The name was inspired not, as I had assumed, by the fact that hedgehogs are just really cute, but by a Greek parable that says, "The fox knows many things, but the hedgehog knows one big thing.")

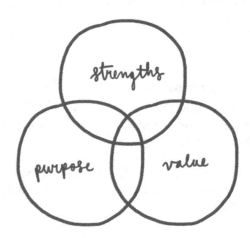

The following questions are from a "personal vision" exercise that Amy designed based on the Hedgehog Concept (printed with her permission). Answer them to get clear on what your personal vision/ North Star is. In other words, if you were a hedgehog, what "one big thing" would you know about yourself?

Step 1: What can you be best at in the world?

- ◆ Is there anything you feel you were simply born to do?
- ◆ Are there things that impress others, but you take for granted?
- ◆ What are the areas that people say, "Wow, you are really great at this"?
- ◆ Are there skills that seem to come easy to you while others often struggle?

Step 2: What are your passions?

- ◆ What are those things that you absolutely love doing?
- ◆ What are those activities where you lose track of time?
- ◆ What gives you energy?
- ◆ What do you love to teach others?
- ◆ What would you do even if you weren't going to get paid?
- ◆ What are the things you brag about the most or the stories you retell the most?

Step 3: How can you add value to other people's lives?

- ◆ How do you add value to other people's lives? By solving their problems? By entertaining and delighting them?
- ◆ Who can benefit from what you're offering?

What is your North Star? Remember, your focus can change over the course of your life. What is the direction you will set off in now?

Make a list of projects and activities that you could try ASAP with the opportunities, experience, and resources currently available to you. Think of them as little experiments based on what you know about yourself. They might be a breadcrumb that serendipitously leads you to something else, or they might be a dead end. Either way, you will have explored an option and gained valuable experience and understanding. The more you learn about yourself, what you're good at, and what you're passionate about, the more open you'll be to random (or seemingly random) little opportunities that pop up in your life.

The North Star statement in practice

Rowena Tsai is a productivity and self-care YouTuber as well as the host and co-producer of the skincare and beauty channel *Beauty Within*. If you open up her life dashboard in Notion, you'll find her North Star statement front and center: "Creating meaningful, positive, and uplifting content to give hope and help others be their best and most productive selves, so that they can find meaning in what is truly essential."

This North Star has guided Rowena since the start of her YouTube journey. "I went through a rough patch when I was younger. After coming out of it— *crawling* out of it—I decided that if I can just help my younger self to feel more understood, if I can inspire her to dream more and to not feel alone for wanting to pursue a different career path, then I've succeeded." With this in mind, she crafted a statement to encapsulate what it is that she wants to accomplish through her work on YouTube and elsewhere.

"It is what got me to sit down and record my first video and it is what has encouraged me to continue creating content when I may be burned out or when I lose sight of what it is that I want to do." Just like the actual North Star remains in the sky even when dark clouds or tree branches obscure it, Rowena's North Star is always there. Every time she opens a video with her signature greeting—"Hello sweetest potatoes!"—it reminds her of her purpose of sharing inspiration and kindness with the world. And if she ever loses sight of it, her loved ones can point it out to her again—"This is why you started, and I think you're doing a great job."

Chapter 3

Setting Goals
That Work

Systems-Based SMART Goals

There are many ways to define what a "goal" is. Ask one person to tell you what their goals are, and they'll give you their thirty-seven-step plan to running a marathon in six months. Ask another and they'll tell you that their goal is simply "to be happy." There are professional goals, sales goals, health goals, personal goals, #lifegoals...

For our purposes, when we talk about goals, let's start with the popular SMART acronym. SMART goals are *Specific, Measurable, Attainable, Relevant, and Time-bound.* In other words, a SMART goal is clearly defined, you'll know exactly when it has been achieved, you can realistically meet it, it applies to your bigger life goals, and there is a deadline.

Let's also make sure that we're making a distinction between *systems* and goals. If a goal is a target outcome, then a system can be thought of as the process you follow to get there. Since outcomes aren't always entirely under your control, it can be better to focus on systems when you're setting personal goals. Here's an example:

Let's say my goal is to reach 1,000 YouTube subscribers by the end of the year.

- ❖ Is it specific? Yup, I have a specific number in mind.

- ❖ Is it measurable? Yes, by the subscriber count.

- ❖ Attainable? Sure, anything is possible on the internet!

- ❖ Relevant? Yes, because my larger goal is to share my creative work with an online audience.

- ❖ Time-bound? I need to meet this goal by 12:00 a.m., January 1st on the dot.

This goal is a SMART goal, but as you might know if you've tried to establish an online presence, subscriber counts are not entirely under your control. The SMART goal doesn't account for the whims of the YouTube algorithm, internet trends, or simple luck.

If the big goal is to present my work to an online audience, what is the system that will get me to that?

I will get my YouTube channel to 1,000 subscribers. → I will take a video editing course in order to design and launch my channel by December 31st, and then post a minimum of one video per week over the course of the year.

- ◆ *Is it specific?* Yup, I know exactly what I need to do.
- ◆ *Is it measurable?* Yes, by my completion of the course and the number of videos I upload.

- *Attainable?* Yes, I know I have enough free time to complete these tasks.
- *Relevant?* Yes, because my larger goal is to share my creative work with an online audience.
- *Time-bound?* Yes, I need to finish the course by a specific date, and then continue to upload at a specific frequency.

Other examples:

- *I will bench press 100 lbs.* → I will find a weightlifting class I enjoy and schedule that for a minimum of three times per week.
- *I will raise my grade in Organic Chemistry to a 95 percent.* → I will complete my weekly problem sets on Tuesday evenings and attend the bi-monthly group review sessions with a friend.

Notice that *these* goals focus on sustainable, important improvements. Improve your videography skills and build consistency, rather than focusing on the often-fickle subscriber count. Find a way to build and enjoy an exercise habit, rather than focusing on the weight you're lifting or the number on the scale. Establish good study habits rather than anxiously checking to see how your grade has changed.

Systems-based goals can be a lot more satisfying to work on than outcome-based goals. You don't have to wait until you've hit the magic number to celebrate—you celebrate each week that you make a video, each time you attend a class, and each time that you get your homework done before the last minute. Who wouldn't want to celebrate more often?

By the end of your goal period, you may have found that you "accidentally" achieved the outcome anyway by simply focusing on the steps that it takes to get there. And even if you don't reach that precise target, you'll likely have gained something more valuable than having exactly 1,000 subscribers or bench pressing exactly 100 lbs.—you'll have *long-lasting* habits.

Breaking Down Goals

Breaking down a long-term goal into bite-sized chunks will make it much more manageable. For example, I already started to break down my example goal of setting up a YouTube channel. First, I need to learn video editing, then I can design my channel, and then I can start posting videos. But even that can be clarified further—what can I do *each day* to achieve this goal?

Basically, you'll need to:

1. Define clear milestones and systems
2. Schedule them (while paying attention to your other commitments)
3. Make a plan, on a daily basis, for how you can make progress toward the current milestone

Let's look at an example:

Say it's October 1st and you've got three months to launch the channel with your introduction video. You're not sure exactly what you need to launch a YouTube channel, so you'll complete the "quickstart guide to YouTube" Creator Academy course in October and design the necessary graphics for your channel. In November, you'll focus on learning how to edit videos using an online course you found. During December, it's all systems go for content creation. You want to have one video published when your channel launches, and one ready to go for the week after, with at least fifteen content ideas ready for the next few months.

- *October*: This month is a light one, and you know you'll be busy with work and traveling during the last week, so you complete the Creator Academy lessons in the first week and work on graphic design during the third week.

- *November*: The video editing course has twelve hours' worth of content, so you set aside three hours per week for watching it. You'll probably need to pause and practice the skills, so you budget six hours per week to be on the safe side.

- *December*: You didn't quite finish the course in November, but you want to stay on track with creating your first videos, so you decide to just skip those last few. You'll reference them if you need to, but otherwise you feel ready to go. Week one, you'll scour the internet to see what topics are trending in your niche and put together a list of video topics that interest you. Week two, you'll film both of your videos, setting aside plenty of time to warm up to talking to a camera! That leaves two weeks for you to edit these videos, which will probably take a while since you're just picking up the skills.

After that, you set a monthly goal for the rest of the year to create four videos to stay on top of your upload schedule, and you also schedule monthly brainstorming sessions in order to refresh your content ideas list.

At the start of each week, you'll take a look at what you need to accomplish that week and roughly schedule that in. You can shuffle things around later, of course, but by giving it a place on your calendar, rather than just tacking it onto your already long to-do list, you'll make sure that you can realistically get it done.

Along the way, you'll probably find that these mini-goals take more or less time than you'd budgeted for, and that's OK! It's hard to know how long the steps will take, especially if it's something you've never done before (as big goals often are) but having any sort of general outline will help you to stay on track and keep moving forward.

These three steps apply to goals you might set in any area of your life:

- ❖ Writing a paper for school? Jot down the steps you'll need to take in gathering articles, reading and annotating, outlining, talking to your professor, writing, editing, etc. Count out how many weeks you have left until the deadline, and schedule checkpoints, making sure to include buffer time for when things inevitably take longer than planned. Commit to putting in consistent work, say, every Tuesday morning when you know you have a few quiet hours to focus. Block that off on your calendar and check in at the start of each week to schedule in any extra time you'll need to make sure you're meeting your writing checkpoints.

- ❖ Dream of learning how to cook? Pick a favorite cookbook and bookmark some basic recipes that require you to learn new skills and techniques. Set aside one evening each week when you are generally free to prepare one of the recipes and set a reminder on your phone to check what ingredients you'll need before you head to the grocery store on Saturday. Bon appétit!

- ❖ Striving to put $3,000 toward savings this year? Alright, that's $250 a month. See if you can make an automatic deposit into your savings account each month and look through your monthly expenses to see where you can trim off enough to meet your monthly milestones by canceling subscriptions, finding cheaper alternatives, or limiting going out. Each month, review the commitment you've made to yourself and check your progress on the savings goal.

- ❖ Want to deepen your friendships? You might make it a goal to get together with a friend group at least once a month. Brainstorm some traditions you can start and be the one to take initiative and put something on the calendar.

In order to meet her work goals at a property management company, **KATIE** breaks them down into smaller targets. If she needs to get a certain number of properties over the course of the year, how many meetings and clients are needed every quarter? Month? Week?

When you're in the middle of planning out a goal, it's easy to develop tunnel vision and forget that you're probably juggling multiple other commitments and responsibilities at the same time. Making a short film? Yeah, sounds easy! You've got your twelve-week plan with all of the steps laid out, from scripting and casting, to shooting and editing... Until you remember that you've also got final exams coming up, work shifts on the weekends, and, oh, you promised you'd bake lemon bars for that one fundraiser. What was it for again?

Maintain a holistic view of your schedule and make sure that you don't take on too many goals at the same time. Remember: "if it's not a hell yes, it's a no." Pick only those few projects and goals that resonate with you completely, and remember that you can work on other goals once you finish your current ones. You *can't* give your best effort if you're overwhelmed, and you *don't* need to have goals in every area of your life.

Technically, "priorities" is an oxymoron! How can there be more than one "most important thing"? SHIVANI likes to keep her goals simple by focusing on one thing at a time. For example, when she was trying to grow her YouTube channel, she tracked her daily progress by checking off a box in a grid every day that she put some work into her channel.

The process of breaking down a goal into monthly and weekly milestones might be when you realize that it's a bit more than you bargained for. Be honest with yourself about what you can accomplish in the amount of time that you have, and find a middle ground, if needed, between where you are now and where you want to be ideally. Is your ultimate goal to read one book per week? If you haven't been reading at all, that might be a recipe for whiplash, so try starting with just one book per month. Establishing a habit and accomplishing a smaller goal will motivate you to continue, and you'll soon be able to gradually pick up the pace.

On the other hand, it is said that "Most people overestimate what they can do in one year and underestimate what they can do in ten years" (this quote is usually attributed to Bill Gates). This holds true even when you change the time scale—you overestimate what you can do in a day underestimate what you can do in three months. Basically, we tend to load up our plates in the short term until we are completely frazzled, but we fail to recognize what is possible through a long stretch of consistent, measured effort. So keep this in mind when you set your goal: you can accomplish some incredible things with enough time, but it's a marathon, not a sprint.

One of **MAWADDA**'s goals for 2020 was to learn Korean. She made this specific by breaking it down into milestones and actions like understanding simple everyday Korean expressions and being able to introduce herself, reaching level A1, completing units one and two of a study guide, watching Korean dramas, and listening to Korean music. She referenced these yearly goals in order to set monthly targets (e.g., completing fifteen lessons from the study guide). A clear goal like this can easily be scheduled into a weekly plan.

Your focus on your different categories of goals is likely to shift over the course of your life, and that's OK! When **SHRUTI** shared with me her monthly and yearly goals, they were mainly academic because of the pressure she was experiencing in college. Her weekly targets, as a result, were simply to get that week's assignments done. You don't have to force yourself to spread your focus across all areas of your life 100 percent of the time, and you can adapt to different circumstances that demand your attention.

Let's Review

◆ **Specific**: There is no ambiguity to your goal, you know exactly what you want to achieve.

◆ **Measurable**: You can break the goal down into smaller, quantifiable, and time-bound milestones.

◆ **Attainable**: It's a reasonable goal, and you've confirmed that it can be achieved by estimating how much time it will take.

◆ **Relevant**: Will this goal really bring you toward your life vision? Your time and energy are limited, so be very careful about what you choose to spend them on.

◆ **Time-bound**: You've scheduled a date to achieve the goal by or to check in with your progress if it's incomplete.

And let's add one more...

◆ **Systems-based**: The goal focuses more on the steps that are under your control, rather than an arbitrary final outcome.

How big should you set your goals? They say, "Aim for the moon and you'll land among the stars!" But then they also say, "Set practical SMART goals." Which one is it? Who are "they" and why can't they give us clear instructions?

In his book *Smarter, Faster, Better*, Charles Duhigg argues that we need to simultaneously set SMART goals *and* "stretch" goals, or goals that push on our comfort zones and perhaps even border on fantasies. You see, people who only set SMART goals are more likely to become complacent. They're less flexible and can become obsessed with reaching their initial target, even if it's no longer the best course of action. Stretch goals, on the other hand, can be paralyzing on their own. How do you even start on something that feels impossible?

Duhigg's answer? Combine the two! Set aspirational stretch goals (like getting to the moon) that inspire you to dream big and think innovatively, and then set short-term SMART goals that get you incrementally closer to landing there. That's why, at the beginning of the book, we started with your big life vision and put together a vision board. That's your moon. You don't need to have a clear plan for how to get there, you just need to have your sights on it to inspire you while you focus on the short term.

Now it's your turn to try! Refer to your life vision, your vision board, your North Star, whatever strikes your fancy, and pick a big goal you'd like to achieve. Make sure it checks off the characteristics of a good goal. Is it specific? Can you break it down into measurable steps? Is it actually attainable? Is it relevant to your life vision? And is it systems- rather than outcome-based? Next, zoom in to the monthly level to set realistic milestones, and create a rough plan of what can be done each week.

_____

_____

_____

_____

_____

_____

_____

Chapter 4

Planning & Reviewing (Adjusting & Repeating)

Yearly Planning

Every December, there's a lot of pressure to enter the new year armed with a whole slew of goals in every category of life. Yearly goal-setting can feel pretty overwhelming because there is so much time to fill and so many things you could fill it with. How could you possibly decide how to spend the next twelve months of your life? Plus, what if your dreams and priorities change completely over the course of the year and the goal you were totally committed to on December 31st feels all wrong by April?

If you really *want* to set a goal for the year, keep the pressure on yourself low. There's nothing wrong with adjusting your goal or pivoting to a brand-new one over the course of the next 365 days. After all, if you are sure that you want to let go of the goal because it no longer aligns with your desires, you'll do yourself a favor by not sinking any more time and energy into it. Even if you didn't get the outcome that you were expecting from the goal, you probably learned something valuable from the experience and you'll now be armed with information to help you set better future goals.

If yearly goals are *not* your jam, you do you! There's no rule that says you have to follow the calendar and set a goal that you will work on for the next twelve months, not a day more or less. Perhaps instead, you could pick a three-month project to start with, see how that goes and then pick a project for the next three months, like following a trail of breadcrumbs.

Try picking a theme for the year—something you want to learn, something to work on, an area of life to improve, a quality you want to embody, a mantra to remember. In the past, my themes have been "simplify" and "boldness." Each month, make sure you are taking some action to live your theme, no matter how small.

grow EVOLVE
balance
SIMPLIFY kindness
TRAVEL adventure HEALTH COURAGE
simplify BOLD joy
FAMILY creativity LOVE
gentle HAPPINESS

The end of the year is a good time to slow down, celebrate the year behind you, take stock of where you're at, and decide how you want to move forward. For you, that might mean setting clear yearly goals because you know exactly what you want to achieve and how you're going to do that. It could also mean simply sitting down to conduct a review of your life. Let's talk about how to do that.

Reviewing

As important as it is to take action, it's also important to pause regularly to evaluate where you're at.

PAUSING + ACTION = *thoughtful progress*

At the end of a month, quarter, or year, or just when you're feeling a bit scattered, here's how you can conduct a review of your own.

1. *Put it on your calendar.* This is an important, VIP appointment that you make with yourself!
2. *Make it a special event.* Visit a coffee shop you don't normally go to or set the mood at home with music and a cup of tea. Set aside your day-to-day to-dos and worries and make sure you're relaxed. That might mean closing your email inbox or closing a literal door to block out the outside world just for a little bit.
3. *Gather any supplies that might provide relevant information for your review.* Journal entries, emails, calendars, to-dos, photos, fitness tracking data, journals, bank statements, financial apps, etc. can fill in what your memory can't.
4. *Choose a format that works for you.* If you conduct your review digitally, it'll be easily searchable in the future. If you prefer the tangible feel of paper, consider setting aside a notebook just for reviews so that you can find your past reviews easily.

Use this space to rate how you currently feel you're doing in different areas of your life. You can use a "wheel of life" template to visualize these ratings graphically. How smooth or rough the circumference of the wheel is gives you some indication of how well you are maintaining balance while trying to expand all areas toward a "10" rating.

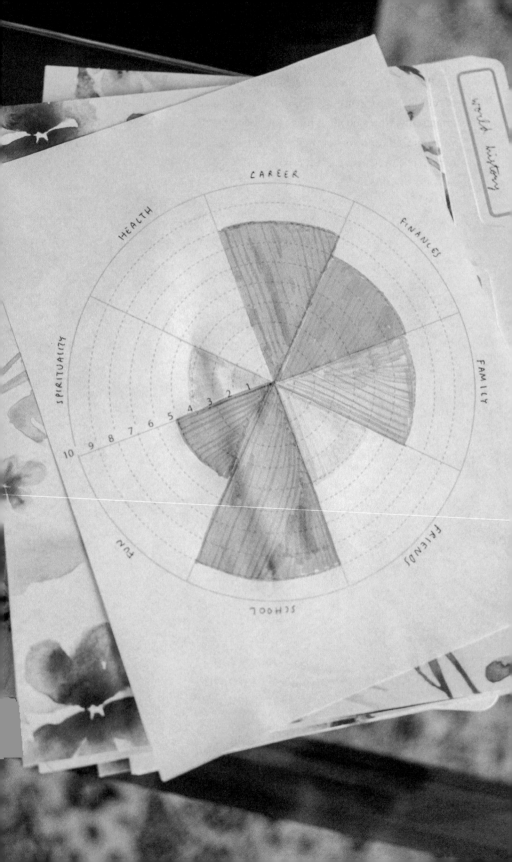

Yearly Reviews

Before you start to think about your theme, goals, and projects for a new year, take a look back at the previous year and write down some:

- **Highlights**: What went well? What would you like to do more of this year? What do you want to stay exactly the same?

- **Lowlights**: What challenges did you overcome? What mistakes did you make and what lessons did you learn from those mistakes? What do you want to do less of in the coming year?

Beyond that, you can design a personalized review by looking at the different areas of your life and choosing specific questions like:

Work: What accomplishments am I most proud of at work?

Relationships: What people made a big difference in my life?

Health: What were the habits that benefited my overall health the most?

Learning: What cool new things did I learn about this year?

Spirituality: What is my spiritual practice?

Fun: What are the most fun memories that I created this year?

You can review the "wheel of life" (or simply assign each area of your life a number rating) and jot down a few notes about why you gave yourself the ratings you did. What are some things you can do in the new year to improve your ratings?

Quarterly Reviews

If you like thinking of your year in terms of *quarters*, this can be a helpful extra checkpoint. If you're a student, you can review your progress at the end of each academic quarter or semester, and again, ask yourself: What were the highlights? What were the lowlights? You can use this time to check in with progress on your goals and set new ones.

Monthly Reviews

I like to schedule *monthly reviews* as a repeating event on my calendar for the last Saturday of each month. In addition to asking myself what went well and what could have gone better, I check in with my goals:

✓ Did you achieve your small goals and milestones for the previous month?

✓ How are you progressing on your big goals overall?

✓ What needs to happen in the next month?

✓ What needs to be adjusted?

This is a recreation of the monthly spread Shruti designs in her bullet journal to get an overview of events happening in the next few weeks.

Weekly Planning

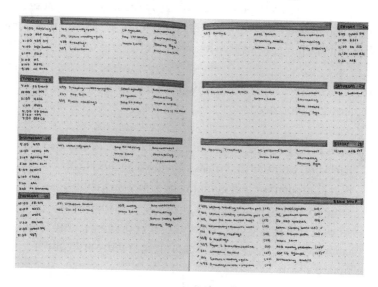

Caroline's weekly planner spread.

A good weekly planning routine is essential to staying on top of things. I usually spend an hour on this, but taking even just thirty minutes to plan for the week ahead will make it so much easier to take action.

Whenever possible, schedule this routine on your calendar at the same time each week, when you know you will be relaxed and have a clear mind. I personally schedule weekly planning for Sunday morning and try to avoid any commitments, meetings, or appointments for this last day of the week. That way, I have a nice buffer of relaxation between when I plan out my work for the following week and when I actually have to do that work.

You might prefer planning on Monday morning when you are starting off your work/school week so that you can get right into the swing of things, or on Friday before you leave the office or your classes in order to get everything planned out before you go enjoy your weekend.

I set myself a rough time limit of an hour to remind myself not to get bogged down in overplanning and move through the process quickly and efficiently. Of course, if a particular week demands more thoughtful planning, I can give it more time!

Here's a basic weekly planning routine that you can start with and adjust however you need:

1. **Start the process with a quick review of the big picture,** whether that means reviewing your North Star statement or just glancing over at your vision board hanging on the wall in front of you. As you plan your week, you'll be focusing on the small, micro steps you take each day, but they should be pointing you toward your macro vision.

2. **Review the previous week.**
   ◇ What were your three biggest accomplishments? Celebrate those wins!
   ◇ What worked well? What habits or practices contributed to your success this week? What made you happy?
   ◇ What can be improved on next week? How exactly will you do that?

3. **Check your calendar** for events that you've committed to and have to show up for at a specific time like work, appointments, and classes, or special occasions like birthdays, holidays, and anniversaries.

4. **Create a brain dump.** Here's a practice to not skip over! Getting really good at brain dumping your tasks and ideas means your brain gets to finally take a breather from holding onto so much information! Can you hear that? That's your brain saying, "thank you." To make sure that your brain dump is complete, you can use a *trigger list*: a list of areas of your life that may require some action to be taken (see the next page for more details).

5. **Review the list to cross off tasks that are not essential or can be delegated.** A brain dump is like a brainstorm in that your goal is to write down anything and everything that pops into your head, with no regards to limitations like time and resources. Once you've got your list, though, it's time to make it realistic. You can't do everything in the world all in one week (oh, how I wish that were possible), so you'll need to question each item to decide whether it is *you* that needs to get it done or whether it needs to be done *at all*. You can mark stars or exclamation marks next to the tasks you consider to be priorities.

6. **Start to schedule the remaining to-dos into your preferred task manager.** If you prefer to have your week fully planned from the get-go, you can schedule everything in right away so that you know exactly what you need to from Monday to Sunday. Otherwise, you can schedule in just the most important tasks and go with the flow with everything else. You could also start by planning out just one or two days in detail and then compiling everything else in a master to-do list to be scheduled later.

How to Design a Trigger List

Everyone's list is different, but your personal list may include areas of responsibility you have at work, different classes you take at school, parts of your home you may need to clean/tidy, people in your life to reach out to, appointments you might need to make, etc. Each week, you'll go through the items on this list one by one and write down anything that pops into your head. *"Appointments... oh, yes! I need to schedule a haircut. Sarah's birthday is next week... better pop into the bookstore to get her that book she said she wanted... next week we are launching our new notebook products, so I need to finalize the web layouts and approve the emails that will be going out."*

Write your own trigger list in this space. As your life and responsibilities change, come back to this trigger list to edit it accordingly.

_____

_____

_____

_____

_____

_____

Tips for Success as You Plan out Your Week:

- Try to batch tasks that are similar so that you can get them all done faster in one go.
  - *Chores*: wash the dishes, do the laundry, replace water filter
  - *Errands*: pick up groceries, check P.O. box, make deposit at the bank
  - *Website maintenance*: update "About" page, change home screen navigation photos, check newsletter sign-up form performance
- Schedule time to consistently chip away at big and intimidating projects. For example, when writing the draft of this book, I scheduled at least an hour and a half every morning to work on it until I reached my word count goal.

- Resist the urge to remove your self-care tasks from your calendar when you are busy. The time you take for yourself is the foundation you need to prevent stress, recharge your batteries, and thus remain productive and at your best.

Daily Planning

If you put in the work up front to carefully plan out what you'll focus on each week and month, then daily planning should be easy-peasy, lemon squeezy! Take a few minutes in the morning to review your to-do list and your plan for the day.

In the evening, review your progress. Tick off any boxes that you forgot to during the day, and feel free to add stuff to your to-do list just for the satisfaction of checking it off. Don't worry, I won't tell anyone. Shower? Done. Get the mail? Done and done! Look at you, absolutely *crushing* it.

Look for room in your schedule to complete the tasks you didn't get around to. If you find yourself falling behind a little bit, maybe clear some room in your schedule by removing something that isn't essential from your schedule and to-do list. You might end up shuffling around your entire week—no harm in that! When you start with a solid plan, it's easier to make those necessary adjustments.

If you didn't complete everything today, *don't beat yourself up about it*. Rather than measuring your success with the question *"Did I get everything done today?"* ask yourself, *"Did I invest my time, energy, and resources well today?"* Even if your to-do list is full of unchecked boxes, if you did your best and had a good day, put a smile on your face and give yourself a pat on the back.

Time Blocking

Time blocking—scheduling chunks of time on your calendar for specific tasks and activities—was an absolute lifesaver for me during the pandemic lockdowns. For many of us, the daily routine we were used to was suddenly shattered in 2020, and the dependable rhythms we once anchored ourselves to disappeared in the blink of an eye. Without a built-in structure, we had to scramble to design our own.

(Waving hello to you reading this book in a hopefully post-pandemic world!)

Whether you're in a situation like the one I just described, or simply looking to use your time in a more efficient and intentional way, time blocking is the key. You see, instead of looking at your never-ending list of to-dos and simply *hoping* that they'll get done with a little faith, trust, and pixie dust, time blocking requires you to actually estimate *how much time you will allot to each task* and decide *when you are going to schedule that block of time.*

As always, you can go the digital or paper route to apply time blocking to your own life.

- ◆ *Digital calendar*: This is my preferred method because it makes it so easy to quickly block out your schedule. With a few taps or clicks, you can create new blocks, change their length, and shift them around throughout the day when things inevitably don't go to plan.
- ◆ *Paper*: If you prefer analog, you can print a weekly schedule template (you can find it in the resources page) to block out your week with pen and paper, purchase a daily agenda that includes a timeline for each day, or simply use a loose piece of paper to sketch a rough outline that you can erase and edit throughout the day.

At first, it'll be hard to estimate how long everything will take. As humans we tend to be overly optimistic when it comes to time (there's actually a scientific name for this—it's called the *"planning fallacy"*). As a rule of thumb, try doubling the amount of time you think each task will require—it's better to overestimate at first than to underestimate. You'll find yourself with bonus buffers of time rather than stressing out because you're falling further and further behind.

Eventually, the more you practice time blocking, the more accurate your estimations will become and the more effective the method will be. If a task suddenly takes way longer than usual, you can ask yourself: Why did that happen? Are there any hiccups to smooth out? Are you just feeling tired? If it's in your control, you can take steps to make the task more efficient or to get the rest you need! And if it's outside of your control, then you know you don't have to worry about it!

MONDAY	TUESDAY	WEDNESDAY	THURSDAY	FRIDAY	SATURDAY	SU
		MORNING ROUTINE				
				SPA 200 Advanced Spanish	hiking trip	
	HUMA 18200 Media Lab	HUMA 6100 Media & Culture		meet at cafe to work		
HUMA 6100 Media & Culture			lunch			
lunch		lunch				
	lunch	dance class			library study	
	ART 1500 Photography Basics					
		SPA 200 Advanced Spanish	TECH 6700 Interactive Web Design			
				yoga		
				dance class		
kickboxing	run				Mor ni	
		BEDTIME ROUTINE				

(time column: 3:00, :00, :00, 4:00, 5:00, 6:00, 7:00, 8:00, 9:00, 10:00, 11:00, 12:00)

Weekly Time Blocking

Depending on how flexible your schedule is, you may find value in blocking out your entire week. The point is not to create a rigid schedule for yourself, but to have a loose plan that allows you to wake up each day with a sense of purpose. You'll know exactly what you need to tackle that day and feel calm knowing that you have done the math and have time to complete everything.

> Your blocks don't have to be super specific. You don't need to label your schedule "read pages 311–326 of German homework until 12 p.m.," then "eat 145 pieces of pasta for lunch." KATIE likes to have big time blocks indicating time set aside for "work," "lunch," "side hustle/hobby," "gym," "therapy," etc. These can create a loose structure for your days that keeps you focused and balanced throughout your week, while allowing for flexibility if a project is running a bit longer than expected.

Time blocking comes especially in handy when tackling overwhelming goals. If you're starting a big project that's a little unclear to you, setting aside chunks of time to work on it can help to push past that initial uncertainty.

Say you have an itch to produce an album of original songs, but you have no idea where to start. Should you learn music production software? Look for bandmates? Design t-shirts? Write a song? Go for a walk to find inspiration? If you allow yourself to become paralyzed by what you don't know, you'll never bring your multi-platinum-selling creation to life. Even if you have no idea what you're doing, you can get started by setting aside a few half-hour blocks this week (you can label them simply "work on album") and commit to sitting down at your computer to do *something*. Google "how to write an album," watch vlogs from independent music producers, find out what production software is in your budget, etc. As you do more research, the next steps will gradually become clearer and you'll be able to put together a solid plan. But the very first thing that needs to happen is that you get your butt in the chair and start working.

You could also go through the exercise of blocking out a hypothetical week to get an idea of what an "ideal" week would look like for you. Of course, in real life, each week poses unique challenges to adapt to, but you can refer to this ideal week to help you stay on track.

set aside time for your dreams.

Daily Time Blocking

In the morning, or before you go to sleep, you can draft a plan for how you'll spend the upcoming day. You may not be able to follow it perfectly, but simply *starting* with a solid, time-blocked schedule serves as a reminder to stay on track, focus during designated work time, and take a break when it's time to rest and recharge.

Time blocking is a great way to manage distractions throughout the day. When you have time blocked out in the evening for responding to emails, you're less likely to worry about it in the middle of an important project that you're trying to focus on. If there's an urgent project hanging over your head, but you've decided to spend your morning working on your book manuscript, you can rest easy knowing that you've got time blocked out for the urgent stuff later in the day.

Remember, though, that the purpose of planning and time blocking is *not* to keep a precise and rigid daily schedule, but rather to set realistic targets, get things done efficiently, and be flexible when unexpected obstacles do arise. Sometimes, you'll need a high level of precision to balance all of the plates that you're spinning. Other times, you'll want to go with the flow more, so you'll leave lots of room for spontaneity in your schedule. It's all about striking that balance that helps you feel your best.

Schultage: KW-11

Montag

1. 7:45 - 8:45 · Englisch Lernzettel erstellen ✓
2. 8:50 - 9:50 · Englisch Lernzettel erstellen ✓
3. 10:10 - 11:10 · Englisch Lernzettel erstellen ✓
4. 11:15 - 12:15 · Englisch Video Konferenz ✓
5. 12:35 - 13:35 · Spanisch Vokabeln lernen ✓

6. 13:40 - 14:40 · Yoga ✓
7. 14:50 - 15:50 · nach Hause fahren ✓
8. 15:55 - 16:55 · Jakob Gespräch ✓
9. 17:00 - 18:00 · Yoga ☐

sonstiges:

· EK IB Präsentation ausfüllen ☐
· Englisch mock exam ☐

Dienstag

1. 7:45 - 8:45 · zur Schule fahren ✓
2. 8:50 - 9:50 · mündliche Prüfung Spanisch ✓
3. 10:10 - 11:10 · English mock exam ✓
4. 11:15 - 12:15 · Englisch Mock Exam abschicken ✓
5. 12:35 - 13:35 · English mock exam ✓

6. 13:40 - 14:40 · Ruhr Talente ✓
7. 14:50 - 15:50 · Mathe IB tasks ✓
8. 15:55 - 16:55 · EK IB Präsentation ausfüllen ✓
9. 17:00 - 18:00 · Yoga ✓

sonstiges:

Carlotta created an iPad template for daily time blocking. She divides each day into nine chunks and writes out the tasks that she plans to do during each chunk. Below that, she records any miscellaneous to-dos.

MAX found that he really liked timetables, but not overly strict ones. Rather than blocking out time for each individual task, he might divide his day into morning, afternoon, and evening chunks and plan out the three tasks he needs to get done by lunch, the two he needs to get done in the afternoon, and so on.

SAHAANAA uses a to do list pad from a stationery shop to write a list of tasks along with how many minutes she predicts each one will take. She also schedules in breaks every forty-five minutes or so.

How They Plan

A few readers and viewers shared their tips for planning!

MARIAH uses a digital guided workbook to plan out her goals for the month, then sits down every Sunday to split those goals into manageable chunks for each week. She'll input those tasks into her Trello board, where she has columns for tasks to do "today" and daily, repeated tasks to be done "every day" (e.g., she's currently chipping away at applying for college scholarships). Complicated tasks have additional bullet points of information within the Trello card, and she keeps track of her events and appointments in a paper calendar.

taking just 30 MINUTES to plan out your WEEK sets you up for SUCCESS.

In addition to her bullet journal, **MAWADDA** set up a whiteboard to plan out her tasks for the week and keep them highly visible. In the morning, she blocks out her schedule on Google Calendar while acknowledging that "Every day, I am 100 percent sure that some of my plans are going to be changed." As a university student, she keeps her lecture notes in Notion, where she can keep track of how often she reviews material.

CAROLINE likes to set her yearly goals in eight different categories: financial (scholarships, credit cards), adulting (car insurance, doctor's appointments), professional (resume, networking, career path), educational (grades, office hours, advisers), intellectual (learning for fun, reading books), creativity (reading, writing, poetry, journaling), personal (journaling, meditation, nurturing friendships), and health (exercise, going outside). She uses Google Calendar because it's required by her university, and she starts with a master list of tasks to complete each Monday in her paper planner.

KEERTHI uses Google Calendar to schedule events and plans out her month in Notion using the calendar template. Every week, she'll write a checklist of goals she wants to accomplish that week and plans out the following day before going to sleep by reviewing the day's progress and prioritizing her tasks.

borrow BITS+PIECES *from different planning systems.* EXPERIMENT, *and find what works for* YOU.

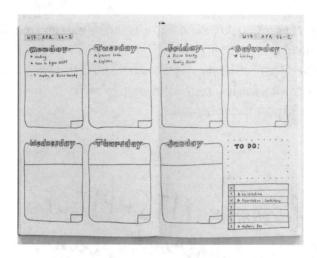

These are two spreads inspired by Ana's planning notebook.
During busier weeks, Ana plans each day separately.

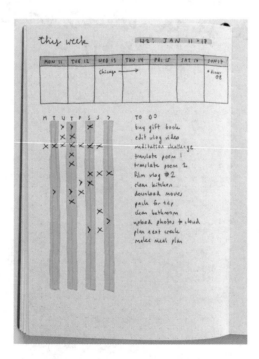

When her schedule is lighter, she keeps a long list of
tasks to work on whenever she has time.

To Summarize...

In a way, you can think of task management and time blocking as *"productive procrastination."* "That's an oxymoron!" you might be thinking. Yes, most of the time, procrastination is what we do when we're overwhelmed by a task or just don't feel like doing it. However, procrastination is defined simply as "the action of delaying or postponing something." When you start investing time up front to figure out how you'll spend the upcoming day, week, or maybe even the entire month, you realize that not everything needs to get done today. There's a best time for everything and it's not necessarily right here, right now.

Planning helps you to make the best use of your time by not seeing everything as urgent. You can feel relaxed knowing that everything is scheduled and you have time to get it done, and you don't have to sort out your to-do list in your mind because it lives safely in your favorite planning tool.

when you TRUST your PLANNING system, you can focus your ENERGY on other things.

PART III

ORGANIZATION

Chapter 5

A Clutter-Free Workspace

Minimalism as a trend may be on its way out. On home decor blogs, vibrant and busy maximalist interiors are replacing the bright and airy Scandinavian designs. The decluttering fad, which sparked books, TV shows, and documentaries (and, in the spirit of full disclosure, many of my YouTube videos) is perhaps reaching the end of its lifespan. As a philosophy that can be applied to planning and organization, however, I'd like to hold on to minimalism for just a bit longer.

I think I first stumbled upon minimalism in 2017. I can't remember when or where I first encountered it, but what I do remember is filling spare moments in high school with episodes of *The Minimalists* podcast. While I ate breakfast, sorted laundry, or drove to after-school activities, I was listening to conversations on how to approach everything from your career and education to gift-giving and home decorating from a minimalist perspective. Eventually, I started to apply these tips to my own life.

The first thing to go? My beloved handmade paper planner. As much as I enjoyed decorating my monthly habit trackers and highlighting my tasks in eight different colors (that's not even an exaggeration), I realized that the cramped handwriting and layers of white-out were making me anxious. I traded my planner in for a bare-bones digital calendar and to-do app and never looked back.

I created simple systems and routines for organizing my life without over-complicating it. I started tracking my time and realizing how much of it was going toward busywork. I learned how to concentrate my study time into the most important assignments and breeze through the clutter. I started to uncommit myself from activities that weren't truly important to me. I color-coded my closet, not because it looks nicer that way (it does), but because I spend less time searching for clothes and wondering whether they're in the laundry hamper.

Most famously, in 2019, just a week before graduating high school, I emptied every shelf and drawer in my room, dumped all of my stuff onto the middle of the floor, tediously sorted everything into boxes titled keep/donate/throw away, and ended up getting rid of more than half the clutter. I documented this process in a video that would soon become one of the most watched on my channel. The result was like night and day. My room felt empty, and my future felt incredibly open. I felt so much lighter afterwards, and I couldn't wait to move on to the next chapter of my life without the stuff dragging me down.

As they say, "clear space, clear mind."

Of course, decluttering and simplifying isn't a one-time deal. Stuff still creeps back into my life. A trendy new planning tool will occasionally tempt me into adding it into my system. But because I know how minimalism makes me feel, I keep tidying my room, reevaluating how I work, and *keeping things simple.*

How to Declutter

Decluttering is not a necessity. There's nothing wrong with a maximalist aesthetic, and it's also important to remember that it is a privilege in the first place to have so much stuff that you'd think of downsizing it. If, however, you are in a position to minimize your belongings so that you can focus better, and you'd like some tips for that, read on. I generally follow this process for decluttering:

1. Take everything out from where it's stored and put it in one place where you can see it all.
2. Go through the items one by one and sort them into boxes labeled "keep," "donate/sell," or "discard."
3. Once you're done, thoughtfully put away every item in the "keep" box.

Simple, right? The most difficult part is probably the second step. As you're trying to figure out whether each item is worth keeping, sentimental memories and "what ifs" are bound to creep in, so make sure you set aside plenty of time for this process and take breaks when you're tired. You'll make better decisions when you're well-rested.

In their books and podcasts, Joshua Fields Millburn and Ryan Nicodemus of *The Minimalists* recommend other strategies for decluttering like having a "packing party," putting all of your things into boxes, as if you were moving, and retrieving items only as you need them. After a week or so, you'll know that most of the items still hidden away in boxes can be thrown away, donated, or sold.

Marie Kondo's KonMari method is also popular. Instead of focusing on one room at a time, she recommends decluttering by category: clothing, books, papers, miscellaneous items, and mementos. As you pick up each individual item, ask yourself if it "sparks joy." Don't hesitate to part with it if it doesn't.

Once you're enjoying your calmer, tidier space, make it a habit to pick up stray items and put them back where they belong, and bam, you're back to tidiness!

Home Office Organization

Wherever you prefer to get things done, whether it's a table in the kitchen, a home office, a favorite library or coffee shop on campus, or your desk at the office, it's worth making an effort to make sure this space keeps you happy and focused!

1. Whenever possible, choose a space that is quiet, or has unobtrusive ambient noise, and natural lighting.
2. Try to keep a minimal number of items on your desk. A decoration or two can be nice to have, but visual clutter is distracting.

3. A comfortable chair is important! Choose one that has an adjustable height. A cushion can help support your lower back.
4. Have something inspirational or calming to look at, like an outdoor view (if it doesn't distract you), a vision board, or some nice art.
5. Choose a surface that gives you enough space to spread your work out comfortably, especially if you're working with piles of notebooks and textbooks.
6. Try to alternate between sitting and standing in order to stay focused, healthy, and comfortable. Before I got my standing desk, I used a wooden board on top of a box as a makeshift standing desk, and it worked.
7. Keep all of your cables organized in a bundle. You can buy cable holders or use binder clips.
8. Keep only the essentials in your pencil case/cup and toss out any pens that have run dry.
9. Have an "in tray" for anything that doesn't have a long-term home and needs to be processed, like mail to read or documents to sign.

Desk Drawers

Look through any drawers and shelves regularly to declutter and make sure everything is where it belongs. My drawers are organized into the following categories:

- ◆ Notebooks and pencil cases
- ◆ Tech and charging wires
- ◆ Scrap paper
- ◆ Office supplies
- ◆ Craft supplies

Chapter 6

Capturing Your
Thoughts & Ideas

Most of us take notes, whether they're detailed biology notes with diagrams and highlighted vocab terms, meeting notes for a project at work, or the miscellaneous lists you make to keep track of the books you need to read, movies to watch, or gift ideas for your friends.

Tools for Taking Notes

It's helpful to have one dedicated place for all of your notes so that you never have to rifle through different apps or bits of scrap paper to find the piece of information you're looking for. Once again, you get to choose between digital or paper tools.

Digital	Paper
+ Syncs across all of your devices. + Allows your notes to be searchable. + Unlimited storage (sometimes requires payment). + Searchable labels and categories. + Easier to read than handwriting.	+ Completely customizable. + Allows for drawings and diagrams.
- Doesn't have the tangible feel of writing. - Might be too complicated for what you need.	- Can be misplaced or forgotten. - Holds limited notes before you need to get a new notebook (this might be a pro if you like stationery shopping!).

❖ **Evernote:** *Free. Upgraded plans available.* This note-taking app has been around for a while, so it integrates well with other apps and is available on pretty much every platform. With Evernote, you can organize your notes into notebooks and notebooks into stacks. You can attach images, web clippings, voice memos, etc. and even take photos of documents to "scan" them (it recognizes handwriting to make it searchable).

❖ **Notion:** *Free. Upgraded plans available.* Notion has already been mentioned in various sections of the book because it basically does anything and everything you want it to. It can be your calendar, your planner, your collaborative workspace, and yes, it can be your notebook. While it's not meant for the specific purpose of note-taking, and therefore might not work the way you want it to, or have excessive features, it's perfect if you're picky about how you organize things and want to design your own system.

❖ **Bear:** *Paid.* This is a newer app that is built for simplicity. You can organize your notes with nested tags, incorporate to-do checklists, and use Markdown to add styling. Plus, if you use it for code, it supports syntax highlighting for over 150 programming languages! It's not great for collaboration, though. At this moment, the only way to work on a note with someone is to export it, send it to them, and wait to receive back the edited version.

❖ **Google Drive:** *Free. Increased storage plans available.* A great option if you already use Gmail and Google Calendar, and you want to easily share files for other people to view and edit. You can create text documents, spreadsheets, and presentations, and upload files from your computer.

❖ **Apple Notes:** *Free.* A bare-bones note-taking tool for iOS that works both online and offline. You can create notes with various formatting options like titles and checklists, and add attachments like images, scans, maps, audio clips, and documents.

❖ **Note-taking Apps for Tablets:** *GoodNotes is paid.* If you have a tablet and a stylus, you can use an app that allows you to handwrite on the screen, thus getting the best of both the paper and digital worlds! You'll be able to scribble and doodle to your heart's content while saving paper. You can even get a screen protector that mimics the feeling of writing on paper! Multiple readers recommended the GoodNotes app, available on iPad, Mac, and iPhone. It allows you to sync your notes across devices, add images, organize your notes into folders, sub-folders, and notebooks, and even search your handwriting. If you're a student, you can get the most from your screen real estate by opening your notes side by side with a PDF or annotating directly onto a slide presentation.

Note-Taking Methods
for School

For students, two popular note-taking methods for textbooks and lectures are the Cornell method and the outline method.

CELLULAR RESPIRATION - AP Bio   10/10/19

CUES	NOTES
what type of reaction breaks large molecules into smaller?	- catabolic reactions = rxns. that extract energy from molecules like glucose (large mol. →small) $C_6H_{12}O_6 + 6O_2 \rightarrow 6CO_2 + 6H_2O$ - energy from glucose releases → heat and ATP
what is ATP?	- adenosine triphosphate = ATP = small molecule that powers rxns. in the cell ⌃ some produced directly = substrate-level phosphorylation
describe the process of oxidative vs. substrate-level phosphorylation.	- some produced indirectly - electrons from glucose = oxidative phosphorylation 1. electron carriers take electrons to electron transport chain 2. electrons energy is used to pump H^+ out of mitochondria. forming electrochemical gradient 3. H^+ flowing back down gradient pass through enzyme ATP synthase
define cellular respiration	- cellular respiration = when organic fuels like glucose are broken down using an electron transport chain

SUMMARY

$C_6H_{12}O_6 + 6O_2 \rightarrow 6CO_2 + 6H_2O$ is the catabolic reaction that extracts energy from glucose. Some of that energy is captured as ATP (adenosine triphosphate) in 2 ways: substrate-level phosphorylation, where the ATP is produced directly, and oxidative phosphorylation, where the electron is taken to the electron transport chain to form an electrochemical gradient, which causes H^+ to pass through ATP synthase.

ENZYMES

I. activation energy

    A. activation energy = E_A = initial energy input needed for a reaction (even an exogenic one) to start

    B. transition state = unstable state

        1. where bonds can be broken and re-form

        2. always at a higher energy level than reactants and products

    C. rate of reaction

        1. the higher the activation energy, the slower the chemical reaction

        2. some reactions (like combustion of propane) have such high activation energy, they basically don't happen w/o energy input

    D. catalysis = process of speeding up a reaction by reducing activation energy

        1. catalyst = the factor added to lower A_E

II. enzymes and the active site

    A. enzymes and activation energy

        1. enzyme = a catalyst for a biochemical reaction in a living organism

        2. bind to reactant molecules and hold them in such a way that chemical bond breaking/forming happens more easily

        3. ΔG value doesn't change - only transition state is lowered

    B. active sites and substrate specificity

        1. substrate = the reactant molecule(s) that an enzyme binds to

        2. active site = part of the enzyme where the substrate binds

Cornell Method

The Cornell method divides the page into a notes column, cue column, and a summary at the bottom of the page. In the notes column, you write down whatever information you come across in the lecture or reading that is important (facts, dates, people, definitions, diagrams, etc.). In the cue column, write down study questions or keywords that you'll be able to use in the future to quiz yourself using the active recall method. You'll cover up the notes column, read a cue, and try to recall as much information from your notes as you can before checking to see how you did and what you missed. In the summary box, try to recap, in your own words, the contents of that page of notes in your own words to reinforce your understanding.

Outline Method

The outline method simply organizes your notes in a hierarchical structure, outlining the content of the reading or lecture based on what is most important and then what the supporting details are. It can be hard to understand how all of the information relates when you're in the middle of a lecture, trying to grasp new concepts and scrambling to get everything down on the page. Therefore, you might want to take some time to rewrite your notes after class in order to organize them and solidify your understanding. Far from a waste of time, this is the perfect chance to review the entire lecture and begin to understand how all of the content is related!

Pick a System and Stick with It

No matter what note-taking method you subscribe to, once you find one that works for you, stick to it. For example, if you start titling your school notes in the format "Class: Lecture Name MM/DD/ YYYY," make sure you do that throughout the entire school year. If you follow a specific template for taking notes on books, start with that every time you read a new book. Your goal with note-taking is to create reference material that you will be able to easily navigate in the future. The only way you can do that is if it's consistently labeled and logically organized.

Similarly, there should be no more than one place for each type of idea you track. For example, any books you want to read should be in one place—not split between a page in your notebook, a note on your phone, and Goodreads. In the same way that you might organize your closet by color so that you only have to do a quick check to see if your purple shirt is in there, you should only need to look in one place to find a specific note or piece of information.

While I use a mixture of Notion, Google Drive, and Apple Notes, they are used for distinct purposes. In Apple Notes, I store personal notes that don't need to be shared, like routines, goals, gift ideas, things to buy, movies to watch, etc. Video scripts and podcast outlines live in a collaborative Notion workspace where my virtual assistant and I can both access them and customize them to our heart's content. I kept all of my high school work in Google Drive, since that was what the teachers used, and I could easily submit my work in Google Classroom.

Once in a while, and especially in the beginning, you'll be tempted to just dump information onto the nearest piece of paper and forget about it, but once you build the habit of sorting it where it's supposed to go, you'll find that all of the good ideas and helpful things you learn will actually be available for you to use, and your brain will get to take a break from trying to remember everything!

Chapter 7

Systems for Organizing in the Digital Age

Organizing Your Email Inbox

The first thing you should do to tame your inbox is unsubscribe from all of the junk mail. Do not pass go, do not collect $200. Delete it ruthlessly. Why are you still getting emails from all of those stores if you said you're trying to buy less clothes? Do you really read every single one of the newsletters you're subscribed to? How many updates do you really need from the apps you use? The more you can reduce the volume of emails that are coming in, the clearer your focus will be on the messages that are actually important.

Whenever I'm answering emails, as soon as I spot a notification, advertisement, or newsletter of some sort that I'm just not interested in seeing anymore, I waste no time in unsubscribing. I used to just delete those sorts of emails, but I realized it takes only a few extra clicks to get rid of them for good.

Some emails are important but not urgent, like a monthly billing statement or a newsletter you like to check in on once in a while. To ensure that those emails don't get in the way of the critical ones, you can set up a filter so that they are filed away in a folder automatically.

Filters in Gmail (and similar tools in other email services) let you sort emails based on different criteria like who they're from, who they're sent to, what text they contain, what the subject line is, attachments, etc. You might apply a filter to sort out any emails that have attachments, so that when you're trying to free up some storage in your inbox you can quickly see what is taking up the most space. Or, you could create a filter to automatically apply a star to any emails that are from your boss so that they stand out in your inbox.

Filters can work in conjunction with labels; a label is just a tag that categorizes an email. You could have tags for different focus areas, like the various classes you're taking or the various extracurricular activities you're part of. Then, any professor emails, group project planning, or meeting notes can be sorted under the corresponding label. You can go ahead and set up filters to streamline this process. For example, all emails from a certain professor can be automatically filed under that class.

You can also archive emails to make your inbox less visually cluttered. Archived emails are not deleted (so you can always access them if you need to), just removed from the inbox so that they're not cluttering up your view. For example, after I reply to emails from readers of *The Bliss Bean*, I archive them because that is usually the end of the email thread. They're still accessible (because they're lovely emails that I would love to keep!), but they don't get in the way of the other, more urgent emails at the top of my inbox. If the other person does respond, the email will return straight back to my inbox.

ALICE uses labels to organize the work and personal emails that arrive in the same inbox. As she goes through her Gmail, she uses Google Tasks to make note of anything that needs to get done.

A Few of My Favorite Email Tools

❖ **Boomerang for Gmail:** *Free. Upgraded plans available.* Boomerang is a plugin for Gmail that allows you to schedule emails or archive them until a scheduled date. This comes in handy when you're working on a project (say, organizing an event) and you already know you'll have to send a reminder email in a few days. Since you're already at your computer and you know what the email needs to say, you might as well write it now, and then schedule it for a future date and time using Boomerang. Similarly, you might receive an email with information you know you won't need until later in the week, so you can "Boomerang" it and have it reappear right when you need it.

❖ **Inbox Pause:** Boomerang also has a feature called "Pause" that temporarily hides incoming emails from your inbox. I can't tell you the number of times I've opened my email to reference a specific thread for something I'm working on, and then I get distracted by some new exciting/annoying/stressful email, and bam, I lose my train of thought! The paused emails don't disappear—they're simply put on hold. You can even set up this feature to automatically pause your inbox at certain times of the day when you know you'll need to focus.

Files, Photos, & Digital Organizing

These days, it's not just your physical space that can get messy, it's your digital space, too! Even if your desk is perfectly neat and tidy, if you open your computer and you can't see the desktop wallpaper behind all of the random files you've dumped there, it'll be a lot harder to find what you need and stay focused on your work.

If the current state of your tech is a disaster, it's worth taking the time to do a big cleaning session, the same way you might declutter and organize your kitchen or bedroom. Take stock of all of the devices, external hard drives, and cloud storage services that contain your important files. Delete things you don't need anymore and come up with a simple folder system to ensure that every file has a designated home and that you can easily find whatever it is you need.

It's a lot of initial work, but once you've got a new and improved system in place, the maintenance is easy and the time saved is well worth it. You'll just have to put files where they belong!

Part of that is making a habit out of regularly clearing out your desktop and download folders. These often serve as a dumping ground for files we need only temporarily or when we're rushing to get something done and don't have time to click through our hierarchical folder structure. That's fine! It's a great time-saver in the moment; just make sure that once a week or so, you delete anything that you're done using, and file away anything you need to hold on to.

When you name your files, make sure to stay consistent:

❖ The best way to sort files by date is to use a "YYYYMMDD..." naming convention. That way, when you click "sort by name," they'll always be sorted in chronological order.

❖ If you're using "sort by name" (which I find easiest because my brain gets confused if files are not in the same order each time I open a folder), you can type a "0" or a "!" in front of the file name to make sure it'll be one of the first files in the folder.

❖ You can create your own naming conventions to suit your specific needs. For example, I use "YT" to name folders for YouTube videos, and "IG" for folders for Instagram posts. That way, I can see my work for different platforms grouped together, and *then* organized by date.

❖ Finally, since the "final" version of a file is often not *really* the final, you end up with names like "FINAL final," "FINAL 4," and "ACTUAL FINAL for real this is the last version I promise." Try to just stick to "v1, v2, v3..." and rename it to "final" only when it's truly the final version.

"YT 20210426 Rating Every Book I've Read in 2021 v1 FINAL"

Here's how these naming conventions show up in an actual folder of mine:

No matter how organized and precisely labeled everything is, your organizing isn't worth squat if your computer crashes and you suddenly lose all of your important files and previous photos. Make sure everything is backed up (your camera roll, computer files, external hard drive contents, etc.) in at least two locations. I repeat, make sure everything is backed up in at least two locations. A commonly agreed on rule for data security is "3-2-1"—*three* copies of your files, at least *two* different media types (one copy in the cloud and one copy on a hard drive, for example), and *one* copy in a different physical location or in the cloud (in case of flooding, theft, or other disaster).

If you're really organized and want to be able to easily find photos and videos in the future (for making videos or photo books, for example), name them with some keywords that you might use to search for them in the future, like the names of any people who appear in them, the location they were shot in, or the activity that was happening. These days, the photos you take on your phone are probably geo-tagged, and services like Google Photos are great not only at recognizing faces, but objects and concepts (it automatically groups photos into albums like "skylines," "baking," and "food"), so adding your own keywords might not be worth the effort.

As a content creator, I have tons of photos and videos to manage and organize. This is my personal photo organizing routine that I do each Sunday to make sure I don't drown in a sea of post drafts and screenshots:

Delete the junk from my camera roll: outtakes from photoshoots, screenshots I don't need anymore, draft versions of posts, etc.

Create back-ups of the videos on my phone: I Airdrop them to my computer, name them with some keywords, and transfer them to the "monthly clips" folder on my hard drive for easy access when editing. I then back them up to Google Photos for a second copy.

Create back-ups of the photos on my phone: I upload them directly to my personal and *Bliss Bean* Google Photos accounts through the mobile app. This takes some time, so while that's running, I...

Clear my SD cards: I check to make sure that all of the photos and clips are backed up and filed away elsewhere, then clear the cards to prepare for any shoots I might be doing that week.

Create back-ups of the photos on my SSD drive (a 500 GB drive that I use to temporarily store files for faster editing): I delete anything I don't need anymore (like B-roll clips that won't be useful for future videos), name the remaining video clips with searchable keywords, and then back everything up to my 4TB external hard drive.

Clear desktop and download folders: I trash anything I don't need anymore and file away what's still important.

Label everything in Google Photos: Just as I name the B-roll on my drives with searchable keywords, I also add keywords to the descriptions in Google Photos (I know this sounds really tedious, but I've gotten pretty fast at it, and it has come in handy more than enough times to justify the effort).

Clear the camera roll on my phone: I'm running out of storage, so I can't afford to keep months' worth of photos and videos on my phone.

Sync two external hard drives: I use an app on my computer called Dropsync that allows you to schedule automatic backups. I have two 4TB external hard drives that contain the same exact files in case one of them crashes (and that has happened to me before!).

Chapter 8

Tips for Students, Freelancers, & Content Creators

Staying Organized as a Student

The best advice for staying organized as a student is to keep it simple. At the end of the day, you simply need to be able to quickly access the material you're learning, your notes, and your homework. This should be relatively easy if you stick to the same system over the course of the academic year.

In most cases, you can stick to just one notebook for notes and one folder for loose papers for each class. If you take notes digitally, you can keep files for each class in a separate folder and refer to the section on file organization to help you name them properly.

Once you're done with an assignment or no longer need the notes for a chapter you already took a quiz on, file those papers away somewhere so that they're not weighing down your backpack, but easily accessible when it's time for final exams. In high school, at the end of a unit, I would use binder clips to gather all of the notes, readings, and homework that we did, and then store the materials in a box in my closet, hidden out of sight. I generally didn't recycle anything until I had finished all of my exams (at which point I would take great joy in shoving everything in the recycling bin and never seeing it again).

CARLOTTA, a student from Germany, echoes the importance of keeping everything in one place. She has a sheet of paper that lists all of her school deadlines, and she uses a folder for each subject so that all papers have a designated home.

SANDRA has assigned different colors to each of her classes. When she jots down a test date in her bullet journal calendar, she only needs to write "exam" and highlight it in the corresponding color. Then, when she glances over her calendar, it's a visual representation of which classes she needs to be preparing for.

Staying Organized for Freelancing or Starting a Business

As I mentioned at the start of the book, I've had experience shooting senior portraits, doing a bit of freelance design and editing work, and, of course, managing both the creative and business aspects of my YouTube channel.

Taking on a project like this can be overwhelming, but the same organizational tools and planning techniques that we've already discussed will be your best buds. Make sure that you've got a system for staying organized from the get-go. You can create a separate calendar for your new business-related commitments, a separate folder for any related files, and a separate email address. Establishing an organized system from the start will make it so much easier down the road when things (hopefully) pick up and you've got lots of clients and projects to manage.

On the time management side of things, you'll need to make sure you're dedicating enough of your time to nurturing your newborn business. As you write your goals, make sure that at least one of them is focused on developing your new project, and when you do your weekly planning, make sure that you are scheduling time to work on it.

As a new business owner, you probably already have a lot of responsibilities to juggle. You'll be tempted to multitask. Resist that urge. If you're thinking about your business when you should be studying for a history exam, you won't get any quality work done. If you set aside blocks of time to focus on *only one* project, you'll be able to give your best effort to each thing. As science has confirmed, multitasking simply *doesn't* work—your split attention just isn't effective. In high school, I went so far as to set a rule for myself to finish all of my homework from Monday to Thursday so that I had Friday evening to Sunday to focus solely on photography and blogging. As a result, my grades didn't suffer, and I could switch into "full creative mode" on the weekends.

you can achieve your goals, too.

Staying Organized as a Content Creator

I get the sense that a lot of *Bliss Bean* readers share my passion for sharing their work online. Content creation is an incredible creative outlet and can become a flexible career that centers around your unique interests and passions. It's a way to build community and share a message, and I will always be grateful for the role that *The Bliss Bean* has played in my life. Whether your content is about personal development and planning, or about the Portuguese language, here are my tips for being successful as a content creator.

Have a Content Calendar

A content calendar is how you track everything that you plan to post. Although you might like posting spontaneously, that can get really difficult to manage if you've got multiple platforms, tons of ideas you want to execute, and sponsored content to create for brands with whom you don't want to damage your relationship.

For years, I used Trello to organize my content calendar (you might remember it from the "project management" section of the book on pg. 43). Trello uses a Kanban board format where, traditionally, you move your content through the stages of production by dragging and dropping cards into columns titled, for example: "ideas," "shot," "edited," and "uploaded."

The way I used Trello was a bit different. I named my columns for the different platforms that I posted on: "YouTube," "newsletter," "Instagram," "podcast," and "behind the scenes" for keeping track of maintenance tasks for my blog. I had a card for each piece of content that was labeled with the platform it would be posted on, any creative ideas I had for it, production checklists, and a due date that the content needed to be published.

My favorite part of Trello was the calendar "power-up" I used to see everything in a calendar view. This was essential to helping me visualize how all of the different pieces of content on different platforms would work together. If I had a video going up on Friday, for example, I would make a note to mention it in the following newsletter. If I planned to film a Q&A video in three weeks, then I could schedule an Instagram post the week before to gather questions.

I've since switched over to Notion in order to make it easier to collaborate with my virtual assistant on planning content and writing scripts, but my process has remained largely the same.

SHIVANI uses a Kanban board view in Notion to visualize what stage of production her YouTube videos are in. Every idea starts out in the "concept" column, and then is moved through the stages of scripting, shooting, and editing. By switching to her calendar view, she can see when everything is to be uploaded. Her Notion setup also includes a "swipe file" (a gallery page that contains inspiration pulled from all over the internet and sorted into categories like fonts, color palettes, editing, sound effect, music, transitions, etc.) and a "deliberate practice" list (a list of skills she wants to develop each day, like color grading or using her camera).

SANDRA also likes to use Notion for planning content for her YouTube channel. She uses filters to view the information that is most relevant to her at that moment. For example, to see which videos she needs to focus on next, she would set up the following filter → Platform: YouTube; Status: not done; Sort by: upload date, ascending.

Keep Your Ideas in One Place

As a content creator, everything depends on *ideas*! Your ideas are how you create cool things, keep people engaged, and set yourself apart from the crowd. If you don't capture all of the great ideas that pop into your head, you'll never be able to turn them into reality!

I like to have one big "idea bank" where I can dump all of my content ideas in one place, regardless of whether they are ideas for YouTube, for a newsletter, for a product, etc. I find that having everything in one place leads to even more great ideas because seemingly unrelated topics can be combined to create something unexpected!

When you're on the go, you can use your "catch-all" (remember that from the planning section?) to capture ideas quickly, and then transfer them to your "idea bank" when you have the time.

After reading *Big Magic* by Elizabeth Gilbert, ANTONIA decided to stop questioning whether good ideas for her YouTube and social media content would come. She now believes completely that ideas are everywhere, and she'll never run out, and is always finding inspiration as she goes about her daily life.

Batch Your Work

This applies to everything from planning your content and creating it, to answering emails and responding to comments. For example, you might set aside some time each Saturday to plan out your posts and captions for the entire week, or you could even film a few weeks of YouTube videos in one sitting.

Know Your Energy Levels

As you schedule time to batch your work, keep in mind that creating content, especially content that requires you to be "on" while speaking to a camera, can be tiring (where are my fellow introverts?). There are probably specific times of day that you are more social and energetic, so be aware of your personal daily energy peaks and dips.

Create Systems and Processes

Content creation is both an art and a science. While it's hard to define the process of editing a photo (you just adjust random sliders until it looks OK, I guess?) there are certain parts of content creation that you can break down into repeatable steps. For example, the process of editing a podcast, writing the show notes, designing graphics, and publishing it all online is probably similar each time. If you make a detailed checklist, you can spot parts of the process that could be made more efficient, and then breeze through all of the steps without worrying that you might have forgotten something.

CRISTINA teaches Portuguese to English speakers and maintains a social media presence in order to find new clients. She organizes her content into five "buckets"—common Portuguese phrases, common mistakes, tips about the language, feedback from students, and fun facts about her—and rotates between these buckets while planning out her calendar. Cristina emphasizes that it's important to post some personal content mixed in with the educational. When followers get to know you, the teacher behind the content, "They feel engaged and decide to enroll with you."

▼ 📝 Scripting
- ☐ Initial brainstorm and research
- ☐ Brainstorm keywords (keyword tool)
- ☐ Write title
- ☐ Brainstorm editing ideas
- ☐ Brainstorm promotion
- ☐ Add promotion ideas to content calendar
- ☐ Write draft of script
- ☐ Edit script
- ☐ Plan b-roll shot list

▼ Shooting
- ☐ Film talking
- ☐ Film b-roll
- ☐ Edit an IG Stories vertical video preview

▼ ✂ Editing
- ☐ Rough cut of talking footage
- ☐ Edit rest of video
- ☐ Beatrice's final look-over for edits
- ☐ Export H.264

▼ 🔼 Uploading
- ☐ Design thumbnail
- ☐ Design graphics: cover image, Stories previews, Pinterest pin
- ☐ Write description
- ☐ Fill in tags, end screen, cards
- ☐ Create blog post

▼ 📣 Promotion
- ☐ Put link in Squarespace link tree
- ☐ Update IG bio
- ☐ Post on Instagram Stories
- ☐ Schedule Pinterest pin
- ☐ Upload to Amara for subtitling

I'm always editing these checklists! I might make them more or less detailed as I optimize my workflows or add new steps if I try out a new marketing strategy.

Weekly Routines

Isn't it ironic that we often put off doing exactly the tasks that would make our lives easier? That's why I love having weekly routines to organize my stuff and get some admin work done. By taking just a few hours each week to get my work tasks, physical space, digital files, etc. in order, I start each week feeling on top of things and I can be my most productive self.

Personally, I always have time on my calendar for the following routines:

- *Weekly photo organizing*: Once a week is probably excessive if you're not a photographer or a content creator or something like that, but I find it incredibly helpful to wrangle all of my video clips and photos every Sunday. I clean up my camera roll, label and organize footage, and make sure everything is backed up (see pg. 122-123 for my full photo organizing routine)

- *Weekly blog tasks*: It's important to look up from editing videos once in a while to get a big-picture overview of what's going on with my blog, so every weekend, I glance over the upcoming content calendar, schedule new content, write captions, check my analytics, etc. Once I've done that, I can get back to the creative work!

- *Weekly chores*: While I try to keep my room tidy throughout the week, a pile of clothes inevitably forms and stuff magically leaves the place it belongs. On Sundays, I tidy up, change the sheets, sweep the floors, dust the surfaces, and get everything back in order.

Note: Every two or three weeks would work just as well. Customize your routines to fit *your* schedule.

What tasks do you need to get done on a weekly or bi-weekly basis? When is the best time to do each one? Schedule these or set a reminder.

_____

_____

_____

_____

_____

_____

_____

_____

_____

_____

_____

_____

_____

_____

PART IV

PRODUCTIVITY

Chapter 9

Minimalist Productivity (Doing What Matters)

I want to bring up that buzzword again, "minimalism," to remind you that productivity is *not* just about getting more tasks done in less time; it is about making sure that you are getting the most *important* tasks done.

Zooming through piles of busywork at lightning speed serves little to no purpose, and a color-coded schedule won't change the fact that you've overcommitted yourself to activities that aren't important to you. I like to think of productivity techniques not as a "hack" to getting more work done, but as a tool to *enjoy* my work more, create *better quality* work, and leave more free time for spending time with loved ones, having fun, and being a human!

As you are setting goals, making plans, and changing the world, be mindful of choosing quality over quantity every time you make a decision in how you spend your time and energy.

- Choose fewer goals so that you can give them all your best effort.
- Choose fewer commitments so that you feel less overwhelmed.
- Choose fewer habits so that you can realistically incorporate them.
- Choose fewer planning tools so that your system actually helps you to be more productive!

Sometimes, you'll realize you made the wrong decision after you've already committed to something, and then it's time to backpedal. Now, I'm not suggesting you go and quit your goals all willy-nilly, but if something simply isn't working, take a step back and ask yourself some serious questions. Are you simply bored with what is otherwise a very relevant and worthwhile goal? In that case, you'll just have to muster up some grit and keep going. Does the goal still resonate with you? Is it in service of some of your bigger life goals? Have you made a commitment to others that you need to honor? Might it be the right goal at the wrong time? Are you simply overwhelmed from taking on too much all at once?

Every time you make a decision to choose intentionality over busyness, your life becomes simpler and more fulfilling, so celebrate the time you've reclaimed!

Intentionality	Busyness
Thoughtful	Reactionary
Open calendar	Packed schedule
Choosing what's important	Trying to fill the day
Saying no (to most things)	Saying yes (to most things)
Room for spontaneity	No time for new opportunities

This is all easier said than done—it can be really tempting to overcommit yourself because it really does feel good to get things done! Believe me, I know. At the end of the day, though, you really have to ask yourself, "Did I work on the right things today?" As you minimize, you'll realize how much more effective you can be when you choose just the right things to focus on.

> "There is nothing so useless as doing efficiently
> that which should not be done at all."
> —PETER DRUCKER

A good rule to keep in mind is that whenever an opportunity arises to commit to something far in the future, ask yourself, "Would I commit to this if it were next Tuesday?" We tend to overschedule ourselves when it comes to events that are not imminent because we see them as happening in some imagined future where our calendars are clear and we magically have more time. However, would this be worth making time for if it were happening next week?

How to Say "No"

No. Such a short and simple word, yet so powerful and so difficult to wield.

Every time I freeze up and my vocal cords seemingly cannot produce the one syllable I need to decline a project and guard my time, I just resort to "yes, later." Problem solved! I no longer have to worry about it, the onus is on my future self! Checkmate... The problem is that your future self has limited energy, too, and by saying "yes" over and over, you're simply setting yourself up to burn out in the future.

When I asked Amy Giddon, the CEO and co-founder of the app Daily Haloha, for advice on how to say "no," I was kind of hoping she would have some magic fix—a spell, perhaps—that would make the word roll off my tongue every time I felt pressured to take on a new project. Instead, she assured me that it's something she still struggles with too. Saying "no" then, perhaps, is not something you learn to do once in your life but rather a skill that must be strengthened over time, like a muscle.

This skill is particularly hard for those who identify as people pleasers, for women (especially women of color) who are taught to be helpful and agreeable, and for young people who are afraid of making a mistake or turning down what could be a good opportunity. So how can we train that muscle? Here's what Amy had to say:

Clarify Your Values

When you're considering job opportunities, for example, Amy suggests taking some space and mental clarity to write down your personal criteria *before* you're confronted with options. This way, rather than allowing the other person to convince you that you're the absolute *perfect* fit for an opportunity, you can give yourself a head start by putting together a list of personal criteria against which to measure that opportunity.

Ask for Time

Your brain needs time for a decision to simmer. In the heat of the moment, you may feel pressured to default to "yes" before you've had time to truly consider the pros and the cons. Tell them, "Let me check my schedule and get back to you on that" or something along those lines. Even if you feel in your gut right away that your answer is a definite "no," asking if you can "think it over" will buy you some time to find the best way to deliver your no.

Distinguish between Not Now and Not Ever

Is your plate simply too full at the moment to take on an otherwise stellar opportunity, or is your gut telling you deep down that it's just not a good fit? In other words, is the timing wrong or is the opportunity wrong? If your answer is "not now," leave that door just a crack open for a conversation down the road or for an alternative way for you to participate with the limited time and energy available to you at the moment. If the answer is "not ever," deliver a firm "no" and slam that door shut.

No Ifs, Ands, or Buts about It

In order to be effective, your "no" needs to be firm and resolute. No more "I don't think I have enough time." You *don't* have the time. No more "I'm not sure I can take that on right now." You *can't* help with that. Keep it concise. The more you overexplain, the more wiggle room you leave others to challenge your reasons and try to convince you. Oh, you're not available Thursday evenings? We could adjust the meeting times so you could make it Friday evening! "No, Jeff, I actually just *don't want to come to these meetings, period.*"

When in Doubt, Use This Phrase

"I made a commitment to myself to not take on any additional projects." How can someone challenge this or try to change your mind? In fact, it's more likely their response will be *admiration*. They'll be impressed with your ability to set clear boundaries and you'll set a healthy example for everyone else.

Chapter 10

Working Smarter, Not Harder

My tenth grade chemistry teacher is known around the school for her many aphorisms and favorite sayings. On Fridays, she'd send us off into the weekend with "Have fun, but not so much fun that you get yourself in trouble!" The one we heard most often, perhaps, was "Work smarter, not harder." This was her reminder to look for the easier way to do things and keep our study habits in tip-top shape. I didn't pay much attention to it in the moment (I was busy trying not to set my lab station on fire), but the phrase was permanently burned into my memory and proved useful as high school got more and more stressful. Whether I realized it or not, I was following my teacher's advice and searching for more efficient ways to finish assignments and prioritize my work without sacrificing my grades. I relied on those strategies even after I graduated, looking for ways to "work smarter, not harder" when creating content for *The Bliss Bean*.

Healthy Working Habits

Chugging cups of espresso to fuel yourself through an all-nighter while you try to crank out an essay in the last few hours before the deadline? Lame. Over here at *The Bliss Bean*, we swear by careful planning and healthy working habits as an antidote to last-minute panic and stress-fueled sprints. Here are a few of our favorite tips for staying energized and productive while getting things done.

Pomodoro Technique

This technique was designed by Francesco Cirillo when he needed a way to manage his time as a college student. Instead of working for long, tiring stretches, he grabbed a kitchen timer shaped like a tomato and committed himself to just twenty-five minutes of focus followed by a five-minute break. Thousands have adopted his technique ever since. The key here is that during those twenty-five minutes you must be *completely* focused. All distracting tabs are closed, your phone is silenced, and you've got all of the materials you need to do your work. It's harsh, I know, but you just have to get through those twenty-five minutes, and when the timer rings, you're rewarded with a nice break! Trust me, five minutes actually feels quite long if you don't pick up your phone to scroll.

Nearly every reader I talked to sang the praises of the Pomodoro technique. KATIE found that when she was able to implement it, the workday went by quickly and she got a lot more done. Each break was a chance to reward herself, to perhaps go out in the sun to lie down for a bit, and to refocus. "You deserve your time. You are worth those breaks. No one needs you so badly that you can't take five minutes. Most of us aren't surgeons."

These breaks can be especially helpful for students because they're a chance to pause the flow of information to your brain while it works on processing what you've just studied in the background. MARIAH makes sure to take breaks after she finishes studying for a particular class. Just like you might need to declutter your screen if you've got a few too many tabs open, she finds that "it's good to close my brain out of that subject."

Take Movement Breaks

If you're doing desk work or using your brain for some intense thinking, moving your body is a great way to clear your mind and figuratively refresh your browser. You can do some stretches or go for a short walk to refill your water bottle. If you're alone (or brave) you can even listen to a song and have a mini dance party. There are lots of creative ways to infuse movement into your day, like working at a standing desk, scheduling walking meetings, or going out for a walk while you call a friend.

Change Your Environment

Simply changing your surroundings can do wonders for your focus and motivation. As helpful as it can be to create a dedicated workspace that tells your brain "It's time to work!" it's also important to step outside of the box once in a while and switch things up. When I was in the middle of an unproductive slump, a friend suggested we meet up to work at a coffee shop with outdoor seating. The fresh air, sunlight, and ambient noise made all the difference, and I had possibly the most fun that one could have while answering emails. If you can't travel anywhere, try setting up your workspace in a different room, taking your work outside, or simply rearranging your furniture and decor.

> SAHAANAA, an eleventh grade student, set up a small desk in the hallway of her home so that she could have two workspaces to switch between.

Get Fresh Air and Sunlight

The cold temperatures and lack of sunlight are a big reason why Seasonal Affective Disorder is a problem in the winter. All year long, but *especially* in the winter, try to get outside for some oxygen and the "sunshine vitamin" (vitamin D). Even just a ten-minute walk outside at lunchtime or orienting your desk so that you get more sunlight throughout the day can make a big difference. When sunlight simply isn't available, a light therapy lamp can provide a boost.

Stay Hydrated

Ever since I started drinking water regularly, my ocular migraines went away for good, so personally, I'm sold on the benefits of staying hydrated. Other reasons to drink more water? It boosts your energy levels, improves brain function, and can prevent headaches. Try to always keep a bottle of water nearby so that you can sip throughout the day. I find that it also gives me something to do when I get stuck on work, like when I'm pondering what to write as the next sentence of my book...

Take a Lunch Break

If you have a lunch break, it often seems like the perfect bit of extra time to catch up on work, maybe get some homework done while you scarf down a granola bar to keep your stomach from grumbling during afternoon classes. I would encourage you, however, to take a note from the French and experiment with a leisurely lunch break. Did you know that, in France, taking lunch at your desk is actually prohibited? The rule was temporarily revoked for pandemic social distancing, but it highlights their firm emphasis on work-life balance. If you were to use your lunch break to mindfully eat a healthy and nourishing meal, enjoy quality conversations with friends or coworkers (read: not scroll through Instagram), and maybe take a little outdoor walk, how might your day improve? You'll feel happier and more energized, and you might even find yourself working more productively throughout the rest of the day. In high school, I would generally devote the first half of our fifty-minute lunch period to eating and hanging out with friends, and the second half to visiting my teachers' office hours with questions or to answer emails. It was a perfect balance that left me feeling both refreshed and on top of things.

Visualize What's Next

When you've got a spare minute while taking a break or waiting for some papers to print, tell yourself a little story. About what? About yourself! In his book *Smarter, Faster, Better,* Charles Duhigg explains the importance of building mental models through storytelling. These mental models help us to sharpen our focus and attention, so while you're standing there trying to convince the printer that it doesn't need magenta ink to print a black-and-white document, think about exactly what work you need to do once you're back at your desk. What's the plan? What could go wrong? How will you respond?

For example, if I'm doing some editing and I take a Pomodoro break to fill my water bottle, I'll run through the next twenty-five-minute stretch of work time in my mind: *"I'll sit down at my desk with my water bottle full and press play to continue listening through the audio and making quick edits to finish the rough cut of the podcast. As I do this, I'll make notes on any ideas I have or things to back and fix and later. I also need to watch out for any pithy phrases I can quote in the show notes."*

Be Efficient about It

There's a great scene in my favorite show of all time, *The Office*, in which HR representative Toby lectures the employees of Dunder Mifflin on workplace safety. He recommends that every hour, they take a break from typing for ten minutes, get up from their chairs and move around for ten minutes, and step away from the computer screen to rest their eyes for ten minutes. Their boss, Michael, comments, "Wow, that is... that time really adds up, that's like a half-hour every hour." Darryl, who is fed up with how long this presentation is taking and who works in the warehouse anyway, says, "Take them. At. The same. Time..."

(In another episode of *The Office*, Darryl explains that he has resolved to not check emails until lunchtime because he read *The 4-Hour Workweek* by Tim Ferriss. I think Darryl should start his own productivity YouTube channel.)

If you take a five-minute break after twenty-five minutes of working, take a sip of water, stretch your arms as you walk over to the water cooler to refill your bottle, and then maybe stroll over to the window to look at the scenery for a bit and enjoy the sunshine, there you go! You've knocked out a bunch of healthy working habits in just a few minutes. Now you're ready to get back to your desk and get things done.

Productivity Methods

Now that we've set effective goals, blocked out time on our schedule for working, and armed ourselves with the tools to make sure we don't fall asleep at our keyboards, let's talk about a few tried-and-tested strategies that can help you get your work done more efficiently and effectively.

Eat That Frog Method

"If it's your job to eat a frog, it's best to do it first
thing in the morning. And if it's your job to eat two
frogs, it's best to eat the biggest one first."
—MARK TWAIN

Productivity consultant Brian Tracy was inspired by this quote to coin a productivity method called "Eat That Frog." It's simple: if you knew that your to-do list for the day included eating a *whole, live* frog, you'd better get that over with as soon as you wake up. Otherwise, you'll spend the entire day ruminating about your dinner plans.

When you're planning out your day and trying to figure out the best way to tackle your projects, pick the one you dread most (your "frog"), and get it done and out of the way first thing in the morning, preferably before you've even checked emails for the day.

Motivation comes from action, not the other way around, so if you take a big, important action first thing in the morning, you'll get a big dose of motivation for the rest of the day's tasks, which will then lead to more action, and then more motivation, and... you get the idea. As you make a habit out of eating that frog every day, you'll build up a lot of momentum and be amazed by how much you can get done when you don't procrastinate on those annoying to-dos.

Eisenhower Matrix

Prioritizing your tasks is easier said than done. Have you ever looked at your to-do list and thought, "I've got approximately a bajillion things to do today, and they're all equally important!" Me too. First, let's define what we actually mean by "important."

- *Important*: having a big effect on our goals or a critical outcome
- *Urgent*: that which has to be done *soon*

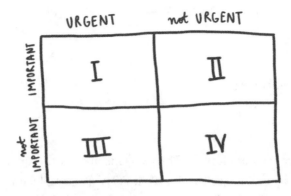

The Eisenhower matrix is a 2x2 grid that categorizes your tasks based on these two metrics and defines how you should handle each type of task. Let's practice identifying these!

- *Completing a report, which is due at 11:59 p.m. tonight and happens to be worth 35 percent of your grade.* Both urgent AND important! It has a big impact on your grades (and thus, on your academic goals), and has to be done ASAP.

- *Creating and publishing your first webcomic.* Important, but not urgent. Sharing your art with the world is a big creative and/or career goal! Once you take that first step, who knows how popular it might become and how big your webcomic empire might grow? However, there's probably no deadline for such a project and no one is pestering you to get it done (a recipe for procrastination).

- *Your team has a weekly update meeting this afternoon.* Urgent, but not important. You have to prepare a few points to share with the group and show up at a specific time, but you know that these meetings are usually a waste of time.

- *Your friend invited you to see a movie that you're not really interested in.* Neither urgent nor important. Quality time with loved ones is *definitely* important, but if you won't enjoy the movie or even get to talk to your friend in the theater, this task goes right in quadrant IV.

So how do you respond to each type of task now that you've identified and correctly labeled it? The Eisenhower matrix method states that the tasks in your personal grid should either be "done now," "scheduled," "delegated," or "eliminated."

- ❖ **Quadrant I: Do now.** You should definitely set aside time today to finish that report. Maybe pick up some snacks and a coffee to keep you fueled—it's going to be a race to the finish and your grade is on the line. In the future, you should save yourself some stress and schedule time to work on the report *before* it has become so urgent and moved from quadrant II to quadrant I.

- ❖ **Quadrant II: Schedule.** You should schedule time to start brainstorming ideas and sketching drafts. Ideally, you would set yourself a deadline to publish the finished webcomic. Once it's out there, you'll feel accomplished and empowered to complete the goals you set for yourself and continue on your creative journey.

- ❖ **Quadrant III: Delegate.** The Eisenhower matrix method states that tasks in quadrant III should be passed along to someone else. However, since most of us probably don't have another person we can dump our work onto (and I would hate to make someone else have to deal with my annoying busywork), I like to think of this quadrant instead as the "optimize" category. These are tasks you should try to make more efficient so that they don't get in the way of your more important work. In this scenario, you should probably go to the team meeting since it's happening so soon and you're expected to be there, but in the future, suggest having these meetings less frequently, or editing the agenda so that they're shorter and more valuable for everyone there.

- ❖ **Quadrant IV: Eliminate.** You should skip seeing the movie and find something that both you and your friend will enjoy. How about a quality quadrant II activity like a shared meal and a long conversation?

Overall, the aim is to spend more time in quadrant II. That's where you're meeting deadlines, making progress toward your goals, and feeling great. Too much time in quadrant I and III and you'll find yourself stressed out, constantly running to catch up.

Look at some of your tasks for this week and try to categorize them based on how important and urgent they are.

Create Time Urgency for Yourself

You know when you have a deadline to meet and you suddenly turn into the energizer bunny, working way faster than you ever thought you could? You *could* just procrastinate all of your work up to the last minute in order to take advantage of that burst of panicked productivity, but there's a better idea. Rather than relying on external deadlines and risking the consequences of missing them, you could create your own sense of time urgency.

One way that you can do this is by employing the "time blocking" method we talked about previously, treating the end of each block of time as a mini deadline. If you've got a slow, relaxed morning ahead of you—nowhere to be, no impending deadlines to pressure you—and you sit down to do a reading assignment, you might accidentally let that small task swallow up half of your day. However, if you set aside a block of time to get it done, say 9 a.m. to 11 a.m., and schedule something else right after, you'll be better at fending off distractions, less prone to getting stuck, and much more likely to finish the task quickly.

On the long-term scale, set deadlines for yourself that are earlier than the actual deadline. I like to do this with videos, so if a vlog is scheduled to be uploaded at 10 a.m. on Friday, I'd ideally have the final version done by Wednesday. If everything goes to plan, I have some extra room to breathe. If there are unexpected hiccups or tiny emergencies, I have two days to deal with them.

Another way to create urgency when there is none is to find an accountability buddy or to publicly announce your plans. Maybe you have a homework assignment due on Friday, so you're trying to get it done by Tuesday in order to stay on top of things. You can text your group chat that morning to tell them about your goal and let them know that you'll check back in with them in the evening to confirm that you did it (and they can feel free to roast you if you didn't). Or you might find a friend in the class and agree to keep each other accountable for staying ahead of assignments for the entire semester. Whoever doesn't have the assignment done by Tuesday has to buy the other person lunch on Friday!

No strategy will be universally effective! KIMBERLY, an eleventh grade student in Germany, found that blocking out her schedule and setting deadlines only stressed her out and reduced the quality of her work. I'm the opposite. My "artificial" deadlines make me work faster, while the actual deadlines paralyze me. Find what works for you!

Deep Work

In his book by the same name, Cal Newport defines deep work as "professional activity performed in a state of distraction-free concentration that pushes your cognitive capabilities to their limit. These efforts create new value, improve your skill, and are hard to replicate."

He argues that in today's digital world, a lot of the work we do is very shallow. It's emails, meetings, and an overall flurry of "busyness" that fragments our entire day into little chunks during which we can't possibly get any meaningful work done. Deep work, on the other hand, requires uninterrupted time, intentional effort, and complete focus.

Because so many of us are spending the majority of our time in shallow work mode these days, cultivating a deep work practice to improve our skills and produce really valuable work will set us apart from the competition.

Newport covers different approaches for integrating deep work into your life. Spending *all* of your time on deep work, for example, is unrealistic for most. Perhaps, though, you can set aside your mornings, or a few evenings each week, for continuous deep work. It'll take some effort—block distracting websites, let others know you're not to be disturbed, perhaps even escape to a library or an empty conference room.

Systemization

Systemization (creating a process for something you do frequently) doesn't mean that you go through your day like a robot, brewing your coffee with one hand and flipping eggs on a pan with the other, then eating your breakfast at exactly 7:12 a.m. *Beep boop.* It simply means that you pay attention to the tasks that you do frequently, both in life and work, and find ways to get them done faster. You might:

- Create a homework schedule so that weekly assignments are completed at the same time each week.
- Write a standardized packing list with the basic items you need every time you pack for a business trip. You might even make a "travel kit" of sorts and purchase a few essentials, like an extra charging cord and contact lens case.
- Combine your cleaning tasks into daily and weekly routines and optimize them for efficiency.
- Prepare a bunch of meals on Sunday night so you can reheat them for dinner on busy weekdays.

Whenever you notice something that you do over and over, ask yourself: How could I batch similar tasks? What different tools might work more efficiently? What's the best order to complete these tasks in? Of course, not every opportunity to systemize should be seized.

If you really enjoy cooking every evening, there's no reason to start meal prepping if it will only suck the joy out of it for you. The point of systemization is to shrink the annoying work and create more time for what you enjoy.

KATIE offered the example of running an Etsy shop. In an average week of designing products and shipping out orders, "Exactly what goes into the tasks that you do? If you had to ask someone to do your job today, would you be able to give them your job on a piece of paper? ... When you write it out like that, it helps you see where the issues are, where you're losing time, and where you could batch tasks."

While not all work can be systemized, even creative activities like writing or painting can benefit from a little routine. Perhaps you have a "trigger" that you use to get yourself in the headspace to work. CARLOTTA always has a cup of tea before she starts working. "You might play a specific playlist, light a candle, or spray a room spray."

Finding an Accountability Buddy

Deadlines have a way of kicking us into action on whatever we might be procrastinating on. But what happens when there is no deadline?

Or what happens when you find yourself leaving work up until the very last minute every single time?

You can create all sorts of deals with yourself and put elaborate plans into place to make sure that you get things done, but a simple way to make sure you follow through with your plans is to get an accountability buddy. Even if you don't feel like going on your daily walk, if the alternative is to confess to your buddy that you stayed home and watched Netflix instead, you'll be out the door in no time.

Find Your Buddy

You can reach out to a friend you already know or look for a partner in an online community. It helps if you and your accountability buddy have similar goals! If you need accountability with homework, a classmate might be a perfect fit. If you need accountability with your YouTube channel, another content creator will be able to relate and offer specific advice. At the end of the day, though, what matters most is that your buddy is committed and supportive.

Schedule Regular Check-in Dates

Decide when you'll meet up or call to discuss your progress. If you can find a recurring time and date that works for the both of you, you can set a repeating event on your calendar and not worry about scheduling conflicts each time. Treat this appointment like it's set in stone, and don't cancel unless it's a true emergency.

Set Good Goals

Flip back to the section on goal-setting for a refresher on what constitutes a good goal. Keep it simple in the beginning and try to focus on just *one* goal so that you can get used to the system of working with a buddy.

Share Ideas

One of the benefits of working with someone else on your personal goals is that you get a whole 'nother brain to help you come up with creative ideas and problem-solve your challenges. At your check-in meetings, make sure you have time to collectively brainstorm on each other's goals.

Work in a Group Setting

Aside from working one-on-one with a buddy, you might find it helpful to head to a cafe or a coworking space where you'll be surrounded by productive people. It's harder to slack off when everyone else around you is getting things done! When you can't go to a physical library for motivation to study, students can find accountability through "virtual library" events or watch "study with me" videos to feel like they are studying alongside a friend.

> While CARLOTTA prefers to work alone, she will tell everyone around her when she's working on a big school project so that they can check in on her frequently. "Did you make some progress?"

Use Social Media

I know, I know, it seems counterintuitive to use social media for productivity purposes, but it's a great way to create social accountability with minimal effort. All you need to do is post on your profile, and suddenly all of your followers become your accountability buddies! You can publicly announce your challenge (e.g., I will work on my book for at least thirty minutes per day), and then share a photo or video each day as evidence of your progress! Your friends can easily cheer you on by reacting with an emoji or sending an encouraging message.

Chapter 11

Productivity
for Students

A whole book can be written (and many books *have* been written) on how to stay productive as a student, but I'll try to condense the key tips into this one section. As a student, you'll probably pull useful tips and techniques from all sections of the book, but there are a few things to keep in mind that are unique to the daily schedule and work of a student.

Make a Weekly Schedule

Start with your lectures and classes, then figure out when you'll have time for homework and how that aligns with your daily energy peaks. If you focus best in the evening and you have a Wednesday class on campus that ends at 5 p.m., that might be the perfect time to trek down to the library for a few hours of uninterrupted study time.

As you learn about your classes and get a feel for what the daily and weekly rhythm of the academic year will be like, you'll be able to refine your schedule. For example, if there's a certain assignment that you have to turn in every Friday morning, you can dedicate your Wednesday evenings in the library to getting it done with a day to spare in case any questions arise. The more consistent and automatic your schedule is, the less stress you'll experience!

CAROLINE says, "At this point, almost everything I do is systemized." History readings are due on Tuesdays, so she always does them on weekends. Philosophy posts are due on Tuesdays and Thursdays, so she makes sure to do them Monday and Wednesday afternoon, respectively.

ANA has to do *lots* of reading for her literature major. If she leaves too much of it for one day, it becomes exhausting, so she instead divides the assignments and spreads them out over the course of the week. If she finds the reading interesting, she'll tackle it in longer chunks. If not, she breaks it down into smaller, bite-sized pieces.

Write down All Important Information in One Place

Keep track of all of your assignments, exam dates, study groups, etc. in one place. You might use a school-issued planner or create a separate calendar that is just for school activities. When you start a big project, designate a place to store all of your materials and notes.

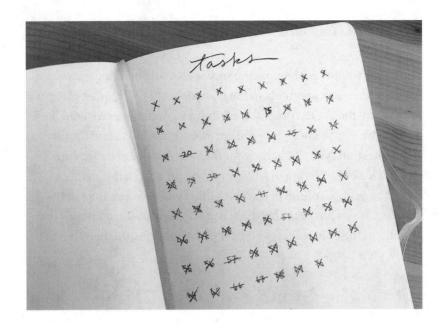

When writing the outline of a paper in Microsoft Word, Joy uses comments along the side of the screen to mark what work needs to be done (e.g., **Research this, elaborate on this, introduce this section, etc.**). She then numbers the comments to compile and color coordinate them in her journal. Blue, for example, refers to organizational writing, while red refers to argumentation. As she completes each task, she crosses it off in her notebook and deletes the comment from Word!

Make the Most of Class Time

Whatever you miss in class, you'll probably spend twice as much time trying to make up at home. Pay careful attention during class time, ask all of the questions that you need to ask, and use any homework time to get ahead. Joy encourages her students to take notes on a shared Google Doc with friends or other students in the class. That way, they can capture information more efficiently and answer each other's questions by commenting on specific sections.

Let Information Sink in after Class

You might want to rush home the very second the bell rings, but try to take a few extra moments in the classroom (or find a quiet place somewhere nearby) to process the information that was covered, look over your notes to make sure you got everything down, and think about questions you might have for the next class period. Leaving class with a clear picture of what was important from the lecture and a gauge of your level of understanding will save you time in the long run. If you have another class to get to right away, use those few minutes at the end of class when people are packing up their things to review your notes.

Use Small Pockets of Time

In between classes, or while waiting for the bus, knock out some small tasks like running through some flashcards, or pondering a tough problem, like choosing an essay topic. Zuzanna, a communication and media student, knows that she can read about twenty pages in an hour, so if she has a spare hour, she can pick an assigned reading that's an appropriate length. Remember, it's less about trying to cram productivity into every nook and cranny of your day, and more about getting work done earlier so that you have longer stretches of time to breathe and relax afterwards.

Break Your Work down into Smaller Chunks of Intensely Focused Sprints

Rather than hunkering down in the library for long stretches of time, schedule short sprints of study time into your week. Set mini-goals to stay on track, make sure that you're well-rested, take breaks, and hydrate. By chipping away at projects and assignments consistently, you'll get everything done way faster, and feel less exhausted.

Identify Supports

Talking to professors or academic advisers can help deal with the overwhelming new responsibilities and challenges of college life. I spoke with Laura Thompson PhD, LPC, a mental health counselor who has spent her career working in universities. She pointed out that most colleges offer an abundance of resources, from career counselors who can help you clarify your values, goals, and potential majors, to mental health counselors and fitness centers. You can also turn to trusted friends who can be a listening ear and help you create action plans to address your stressors. Many of the readers I talked to agreed on the importance of going to office hours to meet your professors, think deeper about the material you're studying, and make connections for future letters of recommendation.

Remembering the "why" behind the goals you set is easier when you find community amongst your peers. CAROLINE, a pre-law student, says that "school is less overwhelming when I have students around me who are passionate about the same things that I am." When looking for organizations to get involved in, she tried a handful and stuck with the ones where she felt a sense of community, not competition.

Stop "Future-Tripping"

Thompson also acknowledged that the traditional college years are often a challenging time and there can be a sense of pressure to make many life decisions in a short period of time. She reminds students that they don't have to decide, at age eighteen, what they're going to do for the rest of their life. Just as an essay doesn't magically appear on a piece of paper, figuring out your life won't happen all at once, either. Trust that if you put one foot in front of the next, use your resources, and figure out how to best get through the day or the week ahead, the answers will come.

From creative side hustle to full-time YouTuber

Michelle Barnes didn't know from the get-go that she would end up building a YouTube channel and business centered on personal development. As a teen, she read books like *7 Habits of Highly Effective People* by Stephen Covey, but that didn't exactly translate directly into a career. After high school, she was faced with a lot of pressure to choose a life path. "Everyone's graduating like, 'This is what I'm doing!' and you feel like you also need to have a plan." She enrolled for a Business and Psychology degree but she's now glad that she didn't go through with it in the end and chose a gap year instead. "I look back like, oh my gosh, I would have hated, *despised* that degree."

In her early twenties, a little book called *The Life Changing Magic of Tidying Up* by Marie Kondo reignited Michelle's love for personal development, and she began sharing her decluttering journey on YouTube. At the time, she worked in an administrative role, so her channel, *MuchelleB*, was her creative side hustle for a few years before she was able to quit her job and take it full-time.

"I'm pretty happy with how my journey went, but I've always said that if I raised a child, I would tell them to take a gap year." A gap year can give students time to decide whether it's the right path for them, and if yes, to make an informed decision about what to study. "I never went back to university, but I'm doing OK!" Certainly, more than OK—*MuchelleB* is now a channel that inspires over 400,000 subscribers to practice "self-compassionate productivity." Her best advice for graduates? She recommends that students look for work experience to see what working in their areas of interest is actually like. "If," she adds, "you have the privilege to do that," because unfortunately, experiences like internships and entry-level jobs are "unpaid positions or low-paid positions."

Study Tips from Readers

SHIVANI, a third-year dental student in the UK, transformed her studying by finding specific, science-backed techniques that work for her.

- *Scoping the subject*: Taking some time before you start studying or trying to learn something new to figure out exactly what you know already and what you need to understand. You might do this by skimming through your textbook, jotting down the vocabulary and key concepts you'll soon encounter, and trying to get a rough idea of where this material fits within the grand scope of the subject.
- *Interleaving*: Alternating studying different topics or subjects rather than finishing one topic completely before moving on to the next. This is especially helpful when the subjects are somewhat related and you can make unexpected connections between them (e.g., chemistry and biology).
- *Active recall*: Quizzing yourself from memory. Rather than simply reading from a page of notes, you can create flashcards and challenge yourself to come up with the answer before you flip the card over to check.
- *Spaced repetition*: Spacing out your review of learned material in progressively longer intervals to refresh your memory, which decays exponentially over time. You might review the evening after a lecture, a week later, and then after a whole month. Software like Anki can do this automatically for you!

MAWADDA uses a Notion database to store her notes from each lesson and then implements spaced repetition by tracking the last time that she reviewed each entry of notes.

ZUZANNA spent two years pulling all-nighters for every essay she had to write because she couldn't get a single sentence down on the page due to perfectionism. Eventually, she developed a process that spaces out the work and makes it totally manageable.

- *Two weeks before the essay deadline*: She spends three days researching and making notes so that she doesn't need to go through those articles again. She then takes the rest of the week off.
- *One week before the deadline*: She goes back to review her notes, plan out the main points of the essay, and write an outline.
- *A few days before the deadline*: She writes a rough draft in the form of bullet points and ideas, which she then cleans up to finalize the essay.

Chapter 12

Managing Your Energy

Energy Management vs. Time Management

When I first read about the concept of managing your energy instead of your time, I glanced nervously at my time-blocked schedules and time-tracking apps. Surely that wasn't all for nothing?

Perhaps you've had this experience: you're behind on projects, so you grab a pencil and sketch out an ambitious plan for the day. Yes, if you just wake up at the crack of dawn tomorrow, subsist on quick meals of granola bars, and don't get up from your desk until you fall asleep on your keyboard at midnight, you can get everything done! Unfortunately, there's more to planning than simply budgeting the 1,440 minutes of the day, because your energy might run out long before your time does.

Time x Energy = Productivity

Time and energy work together like that. Time is a constant (at least outside of physics class and Einstein's theory of general relativity), but our energy fluctuates. We say "time flies when you're having fun" because the minutes of our day truly are not equal. How we perceive and spend our time is influenced by sleep, food, emotions, relationships, thoughts, etc. So how do we factor both time and energy into the equation to achieve our maximum potential?

Daily Energy Levels

Your energy levels fluctuate over the course of the day. If you're a morning person like me, you've got the focus and motivation to take over the world in the morning (if that happens to be one of your goals for the year), but the afternoon is a slog through mud that demands a dose of fresh air and a cup of coffee, stat. Unfortunately, we often have to adapt to the demands of our schedule, not the other way around.

For example, if you're a morning person with an afternoon class you simply can't drop, you can make some adjustments. You can try getting your difficult homework assignments done in the morning, walking to class to get some fresh air and exercise, and fueling up with a nutritious snack and water before the lecture begins.

After consciously paying attention to her energy levels throughout the day, TRIVYA noticed that her energy would drop when she was stressed, most notably in the afternoon when she regularly feels overwhelmed about how much stuff there was still left to complete for the day. Once you've made an observation like that, you can brainstorm ways to counteract it. Could you schedule your most intimidating tasks for the morning so they're over and done with by the time afternoon hits? Perhaps go on a short, relaxing walk before you settle in for the afternoon chunk of work?

Commitments

On a macro level, Amy Giddon, the co-founder and CEO of the Daily Haloha app, views energy as "a pure message of whether you're doing the 'right things.'" When she started her mission-driven company, she was abuzz with energy. She felt "overwhelmed with possibility... the excitement and anxiety all rolled into one."

I experienced this "energy indicator" recently when I had two Zoom meetings scheduled back to back. The first one nearly put me to sleep. I could barely hang on to the words people were saying and I used the mid-meeting break to grab a strong cup of coffee. I managed to keep my camera on and eyes open, but I hardly contributed anything valuable. As soon as the second meeting started, though, a switch flipped. I had been anticipating this meeting all day and jumped immediately into brainstorming ideas and planning out exciting projects. I felt so aligned with the work we were doing and felt like a whole new person (to be fair, the caffeine played a role, too).

"Those were just two meetings," you might say. True! But I felt deep down that my energy shift was pointing me to a bigger problem. Why had I committed to that first meeting and that organization as a whole if I was so utterly uninspired by it? I simply couldn't bring my best self to it because it didn't resonate with me. That second meeting, though, was where I shone. I enjoyed the work, felt that my skills matched perfectly, and knew that I was contributing to a bigger goal.

In her book, *Finding Your Own North Star*, Martha Beck encourages readers to pay less attention to what they logically *think*, and more to how their body *feels*. It is when we run our lives on auto-pilot that we fail to notice which activities and relationships fill us up and which ones drain our energy. She suggests making a list of all of your relationships (from family and friends to coworkers and the barista you see every day), and all of your activities (work, family, leisure, etc.). Rate how each activity makes you *feel* on a scale of -10 to +10. Negative numbers indicate negative reactions and positive numbers indicate positive ones. What's your gut feeling telling you?

Once you've identified what gives you energy and what takes it away, actually putting those changes into practice can be tough. It requires a whole lot of saying "no," making big pivots, and following your intuition, but it's worth it in the long run.

Balancing Your Buckets

An activity that drains us doesn't necessarily have to be eliminated completely—oftentimes, that's not even an option. What we can do, though, is balance it out with other activities that are more energizing, before our body starts flashing the "low battery" signal to warn us of impending burnout.

Amy likes to manage her time in "buckets": planning and strategizing, researching, conversations and relationship building, and *doing* (creating and ideating). Even if she's passionate and energized about each of these buckets individually, she finds that her energy flags if she isn't working in a balanced way across all four buckets. Researching, for example, is exciting, but if it's all she does, she worries that she's not making any progress. "If I do any of these things to the exclusion of the other ones, I start getting nervous, so over the course of a week I want to make sure I'm striking all of those chords."

SANDRA also noticed that she needs to spread her time each week across different activities in order to feel her best. "Focusing only on school is a big no-no. I need to do something creative or learn something that is not required for university." She sets aside four hours a day, Monday through Friday, for schoolwork, and uses any leftover time to get ahead on assignments.

Managing Distractions

There are more distractions than ever battling for your attention. In the digital age, it's easier than ever to reach someone through email and messaging. It keeps us connected, for sure, but at the expense of constant pinging, dinging notifications. Here are some tips to keep both digital and analog distractions under control:

Block Distracting Websites during Work Time

Sure, you could rely on willpower to keep yourself from visiting LinkedIn to see who congratulated you on your new job announcement, or Pinterest to search for inspiration for your room remodel. But wouldn't you rather save your good decision-making energy for less trivial things? As I talked to readers and viewers to get their best tips for managing digital distractions, it became clear that those app limits we can set on our phones *don't* work. To circumvent them, all you need to do is tap a button that says, "ignore time limit!"

If more drastic measures need to be taken, you can install a blocker like Freedom that will restrict access to certain websites while you are working. You can block social media, entertainment, even email, so that you are forced to focus on the task in front of you.

Freedom also offers another tool, called Pause, that forces you to wait five seconds before you can access a distracting website, whether that's a known time suck like Instagram or a well-intentioned rabbit hole like the *New York Times*. That bit of friction is enough to make you think twice on whether it's worth it!

Try disconnecting from the internet altogether! When she's working on her laptop, **MAWADDA** puts her phone away and keeps the Wi-Fi off if she's preparing her lectures or studying for university, only connecting if she needs to find something specific.

KEERTHI, a student on a gap year in India, found YouTube to be a big distraction (don't we all...). While there were certain videos she found to be helpful and valuable, she found herself getting distracted by funny video compilations and downloaded a Chrome extension to remove her "recommended videos" feed.

Schedule Time for Emails and Messages

If it's at all possible, avoid having your inbox open all day long. In these days of constant emailing and even workplace instant messaging, it can be nearly impossible to find even the smallest chunk of unbroken time to focus on your most important tasks. To keep email from swallowing up your entire day, try setting aside specific times to go through your inbox and send out replies, then strive to stay away during the rest of the day. A previously mentioned tool called Boomerang for Gmail can hold incoming emails while you focus on your current project. If you need to open up your inbox to find a piece of information, your train of thought won't be derailed by new messages.

Use Little Blocks of Time to Knock out Small, Distracting Tasks

Aside from scheduling time for emails and other important communications, you can use small chunks of time throughout the day to complete bite-sized tasks like responding to text messages, answering comments, or replying to easy emails. Whether you're waiting for a dentist appointment or standing in the checkout line, there's a lot you can do with just your phone. Remember, though, that it's nice to just let your brain wander during a spare moment sometimes. Your brain needs a break! But if you do want something to do, completing small tasks can be a productive way to pass the time.

Pare Down Your Tabs

I've definitely been guilty of having fifteen plus tabs open at the same time. While switching between a few tabs is often necessary, fifteen is probably a stretch. A cluttered workspace, whether physical or digital, makes it hard to focus. Once in a while, if you find yourself getting lost as you click around between tabs, do a quick check to make sure they're all related to the current task and close any desktop programs not currently in use. Your computer will probably run faster, too.

> JOY, a philosophy PhD student, has a minimal tab setup with just three tabs: her calendar, her to-do list, and a black screen that she uses to make her screen blank when she needs to focus on something outside of her computer.

Disable as Many Notifications as You Can

I find that notifications are like emails—many of them are totally useless, I just haven't bothered to take a few seconds to turn them off. Grab your phone and review the notifications you receive and disable any that are nonessential. During work time, you can go a step further and turn on "do not disturb" mode (while allowing calls from specific contacts in case of an emergency).

As class representative, **SHRUTI**, a design student from India, needs to be available to respond to urgent messages. To compromise, she uses WhatsApp on her laptop so that she's not distracted by the other apps on her phone.

Even if she's not listening to music, **TRIVYA** uses earphones to block out noises and to show others that she's working and is not to be interrupted. She'll also tell her friends and family in advance when she plans to be in deep focus mode. They know to call during those times only if it's really important.

Put Your Phone Away

A study in the *Journal of the Association for Consumer Research* found that just the mere presence of your phone is distracting! Even if your phone is on silent and "do not disturb," *even if* it's not making a single peep of noise and the screen is dark, your phone reduces your ability to focus simply by being in your field of vision. When I'm working, I like to hide my phone behind my laptop, in a drawer, under my blanket, etc. (Sometimes I hide it so well, I lose track of it…)

When she's working, **KYLA** leaves her phone on the other side of the room, keeps the window closed to keep out noises from the street, and works in full-screen mode on her laptop so she can't see anything except what demands her focus at the moment.

ALICE uses Forest, an app where you plant virtual trees and help them grow by staying focused and not using your phone. She and her friends use the app's "plant together" mode when they go to the library to study together. If Alice picks up her phone, it's not just her tree she kills, it's the entire group's! Rumor has it her friends are still mad at her for that...

Be Mindful of Attention Residue

Attention residue refers to the distraction that's left over after you switch tasks, those lingering thoughts that keep swirling around your head no matter how hard you try to focus on the new task in front of you. Some attention residue is inevitable, but if you've taken the previous steps of reducing notifications and checking your email less often, you'll have an easier time switching quickly from task to task. When you take a break, be aware of the attention residue that stays behind if you use your five minutes to scroll through social media. If you use your break instead to stretch and go outside for a bit, you'll have a much easier time getting back to work.

Set Clear Boundaries

If you're studying or working from home, well-intentioned friends might think that you're free to hang out or talk whenever. If you find your productive time constantly being interrupted, establish boundaries for your working hours and make it clear that just because you're at home *doesn't* mean you're available!

Michelle Barnes figured out years back that she's most productive in the early morning. We're talking 5 a.m. kind of early. Her partner and close friends are supportive of her boundaries when she asks not to be interrupted from 5 a.m. to 10 a.m., but it took some time to get there. "When I first started setting boundaries around YouTube, there were people in my life that were like 'Surely you can come and hang out on a Saturday, just skip a day!' But the more that you express those boundaries, the more people take them seriously." And if they don't? "Then that's the point where you need to reevaluate the friendship or have a formal sit-down" to explain that it's hurtful when they don't respect the boundaries you've set in order to make time for things that are really important to you.

How to Organize Your Phone

There are people out there whose job is literally to make your phone more addicting to you. The more time you spend scrolling, the more ads you look at, and the more money they make. Unless you're willing to ditch the smartphone altogether (more power to you), here are a few ways to lessen its pull:

Delete Unnecessary Apps

Be ruthless about what you deem unnecessary. Many social media sites like Twitter can be accessed from a desktop, so do you really need the app on your phone? If you're on your computer for most of the day anyway, do you really need to have emails on your phone? What about those apps you downloaded months ago (and haven't opened since) for editing photos, searching for real estate, and tracking your plant watering schedule? Those can go, too.

Rearrange Your Remaining Apps

You can probably navigate to Instagram with your eyes closed. Whenever you're a bit bored or desperate for a distraction from an annoying task, your thumb knows exactly how to access a stream of endless entertainment. One way to "hack" your brain is to completely shuffle all of your apps. Now, you have a few extra seconds, while you're searching for the app, to reconsider going to it in the first place. Note: You'll probably have to rearrange your apps again when your brain learns the new layout.

Minimize and Organize Your First Page of Apps

Ideally, the first screen you see when you open your phone should be filled *only* with apps that you want to be opening frequently—apps for health, productivity, and education. You don't have to fill the entire screen either. If you have only four apps, that's great! Fill the rest with a pretty wallpaper and enjoy your clutter-free phone.

CARLOTTA put all of her social media apps on the last slide of her phone, set a clean and minimal background, and turned her screen grayscale to minimize distractions.

Chapter 13

Finding Your Lane & Harnessing Your Skills for Good

Bryanna Wallace and Autumn Gupta met in 2015 while studying at the University of Southern California. In May 2020, after the world witnessed George Floyd's murder at the hands of a police officer in Minneapolis, MN, Bryanna created a video and shared it with her friends and family so that they could understand how someone they know personally was affected by the tragedy.

After watching the video and talking to Bryanna, Autumn knew she had to learn more about the context of the situation. She harnessed her love of calendars and lists to design a thirty-day calendar with daily learning resources. For the month of June, she decided to consistently use her time to learn about experiences in Black communities and about how systemic racism is manifested in the United States.

Autumn asked Bryanna to look over it, and at first, the Google Doc was shared with just a few people. Slowly but surely, more and more people stumbled across it, and a few wanted to share it on Twitter, so Bryanna and Autumn set up a profile with a simple statement. Their message spread like wildfire, and they had to quickly cobble together a website that could host the unexpected volume of people trying to access their resource.

JUNE 1, 2020

Hello! Our names are Bryanna and Autumn and we're a dynamic duo committed to the mission of spreading truth, love and awareness. Spearheaded by Autumn, we've created this detailed resource that compiles ways to learn, inform and act to support those in the Black community. Check it out here! Share, repost, blow it up. It is time for everyone to be a part of the narrative.

#BLACKLIVESMATTER

The calendar was simple and actionable. Pick how much time you can commit each day—ten minutes, twenty-five minutes, or forty-five minutes—and follow the schedule. It's a perfect place to start, but the work shouldn't end there. Bryanna and Autumn encourage people to "find a lane" to put action behind their words and go beyond simply thinking and posting about the issue.

Finding your lane = choosing something where your talents and resources meet an opportunity to be able to serve someone

This will look different for everyone. Bryanna and Autumn found their lane in educating people through Justice in June. Other lanes include going out on the streets and protesting, signing petitions, utilizing social media, and having conversations with people in your life.

How do you know you've found the right lane? When you "feel like you're doing more than just checking the box. You're able to pour back into it more than you are depleted," says Bryanna. When your talents and resources are fully utilized, you're able to best contribute to the big goal.

Coined by Hungarian American psychologist Mihály Csíkszentmihályi, "flow" is a state of being fully immersed in and energized by a task, where you meet a challenging task with a high skill level. Some call it being "in the zone."

That *doesn't* mean that it'll all be easy breezy. Autumn admits that it's tiring sometimes. The two of them both work full-time jobs and shift their focus to Justice in June as soon as they get off work in the evening.

"My goal each day is just to be proud of what I've done—proud of how I showed up and how I used my time and resources... After we do that, I always fall asleep feeling happy and proud of the effort that went in. Did I just have fun, kick my feet up, and eat bonbons on a beach? No. That would be fun, too! But knowing that my talents are meeting the challenge is a better reward... Having fun is not the same as being fulfilled and I would almost always rather be fulfilled."

The key takeaway? Self-discipline is a requirement. The goal of the calendar was to provide not just a list of books and movies to dive into once in a while, but to build a habit that you work on every single day, even when you're unmotivated. Your work "cannot come from a place of emotional desire, it has to come from a habitual lifestyle, a disciplined practice," says Autumn. Simply put, you can't just sit around waiting until you "feel like it" to take action.

If you try out a lane and it's just not clicking with you, "put on your blinker and go a lane over."

"It is a privilege to be able to just stop and pull over to the side," explains Bryanna, because the people who are directly impacted by that issue have to live that experience during every moment of their lives and don't have the luxury to simply put the brakes on.

There are creative ways to contribute your skills if you think outside of the box. For example, Justice in June works with a social media and graphic design volunteer who helps them share their message in an impactful way.

* *Have financial literacy skills?* Donate your time to a grassroots movement to help them set up QuickBooks or automate their processes.

* *Speak "legalese"?* Read through the paperwork for an organization that is going through the process of incorporating.

* *Have a car?* Donate your time to food pantries and deliver food to communities that are experiencing food scarcity.

* *Play sports?* Start a recreational sports program in an area that has never had one.

* *Teach young kids?* Use images of Neil deGrasse Tyson or Marie Curie instead of just Albert Einstein in your presentations so that kids can see scientists who *look like them*.

When Bryanna and Autumn started Justice in June, they didn't expect it would grow so much. Neither of them had formal diversity and inclusion training, but they had an idea and the basic tools to get started. Moving forward, Bryanna and Autumn want to continue following their North Star, which is to empower individuals to be part of the solution—to get off the sidelines and get in the game. They want to go beyond the original thirty-day calendar and build a tool that designs customized learning plans.

When we talk about productivity, it's not for the sake of checking off more items off of your to-do list. It's about utilizing your time, energy, and resources in a way that allows you to create the impact on the world that you envision.

Whatever big cause resonates with you, find a lane, bring a buddy to travel with, and start driving.

PART V

HABITS, ROUTINES, & TRACKING

☽ bedtime routine ⋆˚✦

1. BRUSH & FLOSS MY TEETH
2. WASH & TONE FACE
3. TAKE OUT CONTACTS *lights off!*
4. MOISTURIZE FACE & HANDS
5. CHANGE INTO PAJAMAS
6. CHECK & RESPOND TO MESSAGES + DO NOT DISTURB
7. UPDATE CYCLE TRACKING APP
8. CHECK BANK ACCTS. & UPDATE SPENDING
9. REVIEW & FILL OUT HABITS + STEP TRACKER
10. REVIEW DAILY TO DOS
11. REVIEW PLAN FOR NEXT DAY
12. JOURNAL
13. WRITE DOWN 3 ACCOMPLISHMENTS, 3 THINGS I'M GRATEFUL FOR, AND MY AFFIRMATION
14. STRETCH AND LISTEN TO MUSIC
15. TEXT FAMILY GOODNIGHT
16. SLEEP ☺ *₊✦

16

☀ MORNING ROUTINE ☀

1. TURN OFF ALARM
2. USE BATHROOM
3. PUT IN CONTACTS
4. SPLASH FACE WITH COLD WATER
5. STRETCH + LISTEN TO MUSIC
6. AB EXERCISES + PUSH UPS
   → KNEE TO ELBOW TOUCHES, SIDE TAPS, HIP DIPS, BICYCLE CRUNCHES, PUSH UPS
7. WASH + TONE FACE
8. MOISTURIZE MY FACE
9. JOURNAL
10. WRITE DOWN 3 THINGS I'M EXCITED ABOUT AND MY AFFIRMATION
11. CHECK PLANS FOR THE DAY
12. WAKE UP THE GIRLS & GET DRESSED
13. MAKE OUR BREAKFAST
14. EAT BREAKFAST AND WASH THE DISHES
15. PREPARE THEIR SNACK FOR SCHOOL
16. BRUSH TEETH

17

Chapter 14

Practical Self-Care

Self-Care Is a Necessity

Hey, you! Yes, you, reading the book. Look into a mirror (or other shiny object) now and tell yourself, "You are enough. You are amazing. I love you!"

In the midst of all this talk of to-do apps and calendars, don't forget that *you* are your most valuable asset. There's no point in working yourself to exhaustion if your progress toward goals comes at the cost of your physical and emotional health.

In other words, self-care is a necessity. This term might evoke images of lavender-scented bubble baths, cucumber face masks, and boxes of fancy little chocolates, but that is just a tiny piece of the puzzle. Self-care is anything that you do for your wellbeing—physical, emotional, mental, social, spiritual, financial, etc. So yes, sometimes it looks like a spa day. More often, though, it looks more boring. It's water, sleep, and therapy. It's taking an "admin day" to clean the kitchen and sort through your mail so that you can finally breathe and relax without those tasks hanging over you.

If you've been consistently putting yourself at the bottom of your to-do list, you might find your ability to deal with stressful situations fizzling out. Gary Robinson, LMHC, Director of Counseling at Hartwick College and consultant at P3 Mental Health, warns that irritability and panic attacks are two examples of the brain's "dashboard warning lights" that signal it's time to press pause, figure out what's going on, and reach out for help.

Even when all the warning signs are there, many people struggle to accept the idea of "self-care" because they see it as selfish to put themselves ahead of others. But if the frazzled and exhausted version of you is going around snapping at people for no reason, wouldn't it be better for you *and* everyone around you if you took a few hours to get the rest you need?

Just think of how easily your mood can be influenced by those around you. It takes just one comment from a crabby boss to sour your mood, and then one small joke shared with a stranger to brighten it back up. You have that same influence, and *you can only be your best self and take care of others if you take care of yourself first.*

> I couldn't have put it better than KATIE did when she said that, when you prioritize self-care, "You have the most graciousness, kindness, and patience toward others, because you don't feel like you stole time from yourself to give to others."

Remember that Eisenhower matrix from the productivity section? We drew a 2x2 grid and sorted our tasks based on how urgent and important they are. Self-care falls squarely in quadrant II. It's important and worthwhile, but it's usually not urgent. There's no deadline to take care of yourself, and we can run on empty for quite a while before we completely burn out. Here are some tips to ensure that self-care happens even in the midst of a busy schedule.

1. *Pick self-care that matches what you need.* Certain acts of self-care, like the aforementioned bubble baths, are just more Instagrammable than others. But if you choose your self-care based on that alone, you might find yourself no more relaxed than you were when you started, and perhaps even more stressed out because of the time you've wasted. Personally, I'm not a fan of baths. I just get bored and uncomfortable sitting in warm water, trying to hold my phone above the water to read a Kindle book. I know it would be much more effective for me to go to bed early tonight or go outside for a few minutes to enjoy the sunny day.

2. *Make it a habit.* Routines and habits can help to cement helpful self-care practices into automatic actions. You might, for example, create a morning routine that consists of journaling, going for a walk, and planning your day. The more often you do this, the less thinking it will take, and pretty soon you'll be starting each day by filling your cup so that you can show up for others in the best way possible.

3. *Literally put it on the calendar.* I know an hour-long block on your calendar titled "bake cookies" might look weird next to the other very serious and professional appointments that you have, but if baking cookies is what you need today, putting it on your calendar signifies a commitment you've made to yourself. Show up for your wellbeing in the same way that you would show up to a meeting.

Completing the Stress Response Cycle

In prehistoric times, our bodies would respond to stressors by priming every organ to deal with whatever was threatening our survival, like a lion charging toward us at fifty miles per hour. This required speeding up the heartbeat and breathing, tensing the muscles, and deprioritizing other processes, like digestion and the immune system, because we could hold off on digesting lunch until we were safe from the threat. Once the lion got tired or something, and you were safely back home, the stress cycle was completed. Time to celebrate!

These days, we're faced not with hungry lions, but rather with constant daily stressors that are (usually) not life-threatening. Our bodies don't understand the difference, though. The deadlines and responsibilities pile up, our organ systems prepare to fight for survival, but there is never that satisfying conclusion to signal to your body that everything is OK. Once you've alleviated the threat of one exam, your professor just schedules another one.

So how do you complete the stress cycle if your modern stressors are never-ending? In their book *Burnout*, Emily and Amelia Nagoski have a few suggestions. First and foremost, "Physical activity is the single most efficient strategy for completing the stress response cycle." That doesn't mean you need to go get a gym membership, or even step outside. Heck, you don't have to call it a "workout." You can do some big stretches, punch a pillow, or have a dance party in your room. If physical activity doesn't float your boat, Emily and Amelia also recommend deep breathing, belly laughing, hugging or kissing someone you feel safe around, crying it out, and making some art, so take your pick and find what works for you.

However you go about doing it, make sure you're completing your cycle in some way every day. It'd be great if we could wave a magic wand and make all of our stressors go away. "Bibbidi bobbidi boo, please stop stressing me out, thanks!" Luckily, you don't need to make the stressor go away; you just need to manage the body's stress response. And if you learn to do that? Well, you'll do yourself a huge favor. According to the American Psychological Association, chronic stress has been linked to heart disease, metabolic disorders, and immune disorders, among other issues. So put on some running shoes and let's run away from your metaphorical lion.

Sleep

When I was in middle school, I stumbled upon an article that profiled a few inspiring teen entrepreneurs who were balancing school with building a business. One of the teens proudly explained that they're working so hard, they hardly sleep. They'll be able to "sleep when they're older," anyway!

This was *terrible* advice for young and impressionable kids. We know from countless studies that sleep deprivation throws your body completely out of whack. Your memory and concentration worsen, your immune system is compromised, you have a higher risk of diabetes and heart disease, and you're more prone to accidents.

Even with this knowledge, we're all guilty of skipping our zzz's then and now. Sometimes it's because we're going through a hard time and facing some exhausting challenges in our lives. Other times it's because we procrastinated on a big assignment upon which our entire grade is dependent. That happens, it's alright.

Yet, other times, we sacrifice our sleep because we're led to believe, by the social norms around us, that we can't be both hardworking *and* well-rested. You might have experienced this sort of competitive environment at school or at a job. *"Oh, you got seven hours of sleep last night? How lucky! *sigh* I've been getting four this week, I'm sooo tired from all of these AP classes."* As USC student Ellen Murray wrote in a piece for the *Daily Trojan*, "It's the suffering Olympics, and the first one to collapse wins."

I'll admit that I, too, wore sleep deprivation as a badge of honor in high school. But as I started implementing strategies for efficiency, I realized that taking care of myself and working *smarter*, not harder, worked so much better than burning the midnight oil and toting a thermos of strong black tea to stay awake in school. My hope is that with some of the strategies in this book, you'll find a way to get the grades and the achievements that you're striving for *and* get your nightly recommended hours of sleep. If that just isn't feasible, keep this in mind:

"A healthy man wants a thousand things.
A sick man only wants one."
—CONFUCIUS

Self-Care Ideas (That Aren't Taking a Bath)

To summarize, it's essential that you complete your stress response cycle every day and spend enough hours in bed for your body and mind to recover. Here are a few other ways to take care of your wellbeing:

Therapy

Seeing a counselor regularly does for your mental health what working with a personal trainer does for your physical health. You can learn how to improve your wellbeing and have a safe place to vent your worries and frustrations.

Maintain a Tidy Space

In the life simulation video game *The Sims*, your Sims (the characters you control) experience negative "moodlets" when you fail to clean up their space. Forgot to take out the trash? Your Sim gains an "unpleasant surroundings" moodlet and their mood takes a measurable hit. Think of yourself as a Sim. Keeping your space clean and tidy is not just an arbitrary item on your to-do list, but something that directly impacts your mood, so wash those dishes for a +15 mood boost!

Practice Proper Nutrition

What you put in your body has a big impact on how you feel! Perfection is unnecessary (and can become unhealthy in its own sense), so just check in with where you're at and make a few small changes. Are you getting enough sunshine during the winter months, or might you benefit from a vitamin D supplement? Are you eating enough probiotic foods to support your gut health? Are there any foods that you've noticed make you feel sluggish and down?

Disconnect Completely

I don't like doing things halfway and that *includes* relaxation. Trying to mix work and play at every moment of your day (by carrying around your work email on your phone everywhere that you go, for example) can be very draining! When you start to feel that burnout, carve out time to fully step away, whether that is for an evening or a week. Protect that time by treating it as a non-negotiable calendar appointment, and let people know they won't be able to reach out while you're on "vacation mode."

After a busy week of university classes and teaching German lessons, **MAWADDA** sets aside her Saturday to do things that make her happy, like painting or writing with journaling prompts. Blocking off a day "gives me a great boost for the beginning of the week." A few days into the week, she sets aside a smaller chunk of time to spend on self-care activities in order to prevent midweek burnout.

Read a Fictional Book

I was a voracious reader when I was little, but once I got into the nonfiction personal development genre, reading made-up stories suddenly felt like a waste of time! Nothing could be further from the truth, as reading fictional stories can improve our empathy and social cognition. I feel like I have a fresh perspective on life when I've taken a little trip into a fantasy world.

SAHAANAA loves reading because it allows her to escape and experience new perspectives that she wouldn't otherwise get to see in the real world, all while making personal discoveries about herself. "It's a nice way to feel 'at home' in a home that isn't your home."

You Can't Do It Alone

In their book, *Burnout: The Secret to Unlocking the Stress Cycle,* Emily and Amelia Nagoski explain that we *need* to care for one another so that we can all be at our best. We're human beings! We're wired to crave community and connection. "Humans are not built to function autonomously; we are built to oscillate from connection to autonomy and back again. Connection—with friends, family, pets, the divine, etc.—is as necessary as food and water."

When you need a little help from your friends, don't be afraid to ask for it. In Western cultures, we tend to value independence and individual accomplishment very highly. While it's awesome to love yourself and be comfortable with getting sh*t done on your own, we can be *even stronger* together.

When a friend is struggling, mental health counselor Laura Thompson says that listening is the number one thing you can do to help. Start with, "I'm here for you and I support you. How can I help?" Sometimes, though, a person in need isn't sure what might make them feel better, so you can take some initiative. "Why don't I come over with some dinner and we can sit together and maybe go for a walk to get some sun?" or "I can walk with you to the university counseling center."

Autumn Gupta, the co-founder of Justice in June (which you read about earlier), emphasized the importance of having people around you in a social movement. "This year in general has shown me how the quality of my life is a direct reflection of the quality of my relationships." When the going gets tough, having people that you can vent to makes all the difference, Autumn says. "Objectively, nothing changes, but you feel better, and I think that helps you feel more connected. When you feel connected, you feel like you have meaning. You're seen, you're heard, you're fully known. I think that's how I've always felt that my life is meaningful—because of who I know that knows me, and that I *do* matter to those people."

Self-care is not always as solitary as the word may suggest. Surround yourself with people you trust, provide support when you can, and accept it when you need it. There is nothing wrong with you if you need a little support and encouragement once in a while. We're all in this together, and when we accept help and show vulnerability, it gives everyone around you permission to do the same.

Which relationships give you energy and which take it away? How can you spend more quality time with the people in your life who give you strength? How can you support each other's goals?

Self-Compassionate Productivity

You don't often find self-compassion and productivity together in the same sentence. Michelle Barnes noticed that the productivity space online was filled with 5 a.m. wakeups, hustle culture, and "just do it" energy. It prioritized self-discipline and self-control above all else.

Through her YouTube channel, *MuchelleB*, Michelle wants to offer "self-compassionate productivity" as an alternative that takes into account the fact that "we are people and not robots." Sheer willpower and grit don't change the fact that "you have different days where you're at different energy states, different moods, and different seasons in life."

You could read every book in the library about the benefits of self-kindness and self-love, but when it comes time to actually apply those mindsets, most of us are hesitant. It's like the problem of sleep deprivation; we all *know* the costs associated with not getting enough sleep and we've seen the statistics, but... We have goals to achieve! We're busy. We'll sleep once we're done! Similarly, when it comes to choosing between self-compassion and perfectionism, we mistakenly assume that harsh self-discipline is the only way to get anything done. "You can get into a cycle of thinking that the self-criticism in your head is actually helping you."

Michelle wants people to know that self-compassion and productivity, just like rest and achievement, are *not* mutually exclusive; in fact, they support one another. Approaching productivity with a self-compassionate perspective leads to "productivity, resilience, better stress management, and you'll get *more* done as a result of it." That's right, you'll be *more* successful if you embrace your shifting energy levels and refrain from punishing yourself every time you trip up the tiniest bit.

When Michelle finds herself slipping into self-criticism, she'll do a self-compassion meditation or answer a self-compassion journal prompt. "That usually tends to lead me back into either taking action or sometimes just realizing 'Hey, today isn't the day.' Maybe I need to treat myself to some self-care this afternoon, or maybe there's a favor I can do for my future self, as opposed to just trying to power through it."

Chapter 15

Developing a Journaling Practice

When I was little, I loved seeing photos of really beautiful art journals and leather-bound diaries. I was enchanted by the idea of documenting my life for my future great-great-grandchildren to one day discover a mysterious chest full of journals, blow the dust off the covers, and open a window to my past. However, it wasn't until 2017 that I actually started journaling consistently.

My problem was my lofty expectations. In my mind, if my journal wasn't neat and beautiful, it wasn't worth it. If I didn't record absolutely every single thought that went through my mind and every little thing that I did that day, I considered myself to be a failure at journaling! Obviously, approaching what should have been a fun hobby in this way made it feel like a chore. I felt like a historian assigned with the tedious task of documenting my life.

It wasn't until I shed all of these expectations for perfectionism that I could actually form a journaling habit.

I stopped trying to make my journal look perfect. Rather than collecting beautiful notebooks that I was scared to tarnish with the first entry, I picked up any old notebook that I found lying around. A half-full *Phineas and Ferb*-themed notebook that my brother used for his second-grade math class? Just rip out the first few pages, and it's good to go! I found fancy pens, stickers, and washi tape to be too much work, so I opted for a plain marker or pen.

I stopped writing for some future reader. I no longer tried to make my entries interesting or even legible for those hypothetical great-great-grandkids. My journal is quite boring to read, actually. It's repetitive and mundane, but it's what I feel I need to get off my chest each time that I sit down to write, and if future me finds it tedious to flip through those ramblings, then so be it!

I stopped trying to record everything that happened. I'm sure there are many big life events that are completely absent from my journals, and that's OK! I probably have photos and videos to fill in those gaps, and if not, I won't notice. If I forced myself to write about every exciting thing that happened, I would grow to despise journaling. I would rather stick to a consistent writing habit than remember, thirty years into the future, what I wore today while I shopped for groceries.

Once this journaling habit started, it never stopped. I was so much more clear-minded and positive in my daily life when I had a place to dump all of my worries and anxieties, practice gratitude and self-kindness, and maintain an internal dialogue with myself.

A Journal Is a Place to Vent & Learn about Yourself...

One day in high school, a friend of mine shared with me that she had been feeling completely overwhelmed by the stresses of senior year—exams, college applications, and the like. Since I'm always going on and on about how much I love journaling (I assumed my friends just tuned me out), she decided to give it a try during her study hall. After spilling all of her thoughts and worries onto a piece of notebook paper, she felt a weight come off her shoulders, and suddenly everything seemed so much more manageable!

It's so therapeutic to tell someone about what's bothering you, but there isn't always someone around to vent to. Other times, your troubles are too private for anyone's eyes and ears but your own. Worrisome thoughts can bounce around your head all day long if you don't provide an outlet for them, so setting aside some time each day to get them out of your head and down on paper clears space for peace and calm.

You can even pretend you're talking to your journal like a person. You don't have to start your entries with "Dear diary" if that makes you cringe, but you can write down your thoughts in a stream-of-consciousness manner the way you would speak to a friend.

A Journal Is a Place to Learn Life's Lessons...

We all get caught up in the everyday hustle and bustle sometimes and forget to take the time to pause and reflect. If something went well, *why* did it go well? If not, what can be done better next time? Life is almost like a series of little experiments that we can learn from, but unless we take the time to evaluate them, we'll just make those same mistakes again. Your journal is the perfect place to delve into some of those deep questions.

When reflection becomes an automatic habit, we can learn the lessons that life has to offer that much faster. Rowena Tsai shared that over time, she has moved from processing her life experiences exclusively at regular intervals (like yearly or monthly reviews) to more in-the-moment reflection. If there is a disagreement or if something doesn't go as planned, in the next day or two, she'll sit down to think it over and write about it. Just like a little kid goes around asking "why?" all the time, posing the same question to yourself can uncover deeper understandings of the patterns in your life. "I feel this way—why? Because this thing happened—why? OK, it happened because of this—why?" So on and so forth, down to at least five layers of "why" that reveal to you how you can respond more proactively next time.

A Journal Is a Place to Practice Gratitude and Self-Kindness...

Along with stream-of-consciousness journaling, I love to add a little bit of structure to my journaling through daily lists. Each morning, I write down three things I'm looking forward to and three good decisions that would make it an even better day. In the evening, before I go to bed, I write down three things I was grateful for that day, as well as three "wins" or accomplishments that I'm proud of.

Today I'm Looking Forward To...
1. Watching that new documentary on Hulu
2. Having a slow breakfast
3. Calling my accountability buddy for our weekly check-in

Even if you wake up on the wrong side of the bed and feel anxious about facing a stressful day, picking out three little things that you can look forward to that day, whether it's a dinner with friends or just listening to your favorite playlist on the way to work, forces you to focus on the positive and establishes a pattern of optimism that carries into the rest of your day.

Three Good Decisions I Can Make Today...
1. Get to inbox zero
2. Wash my makeup brushes
3. Start my bedtime routine by 9 p.m.

It can be overwhelming to look at your to do list at the start of the day and visualize everything you'll need to get done, so naming just one or two little things you can do to make it a better day is a great way to make incremental changes. For example, if you're in the middle of a really busy week of studying and you're feeling sluggish because you've been staying up late and subsisting on mac and cheese, you might resolve to add some vegetables on the side of your lunch and go for a ten-minute walk to get some fresh air during a study break. Low effort? Yes. Big impact? Absolutely! You can pair up with your accountability buddy on this. Each morning, my friend and I text each other our three good decisions for the day, and then check back in the evening to report on our success.

Three Things I Am Grateful For...
1. Watching a comedy special with my mom
2. Finding a new album to listen to
3. My new dress came in the mail!

In the evening, even if you've had a no good, very bad day, missed the train, forgotten a deadline, and stubbed your toe you can still find three things to be grateful for, I promise! Some days it might be flowers from a loved one or a beautiful sunset. Other days, you'll go back to the basics—if you have a roof over your head, food in your belly, and clean water to drink, that's three things already! Suddenly, the little stresses of the day (and the pain of your bruised toe) seem to just melt away.

Three Wins from Today...
1. Spent four hours writing
2. Went on a quick walk to enjoy the sunshine
3. Made time for a guided meditation at lunchtime

Not every day will be immensely "productive." Some days we just have less energy, and that's OK. Consistently writing down three wins, no matter what, helps you to see the value in every day. You took a shower today? Amazing! Paid someone a compliment? I bet that made their day.

Mix and match these daily journaling prompts to create your own journaling routine!

- X things I'm excited about today
- X things I can do to make today better
- My most important task today
- X things I accomplished today
- X things I was grateful for today
- The highlight of today
- My most important task for tomorrow
- A photo from today (easy to do with digital journaling)

MAX finds that when he writes down the highlights of each day (for example, "Today I had an amazing guitar lesson and talked to my best friend"), it helps him hold onto memories he might otherwise forget.

Journaling Techniques

Morning Pages

In her book *The Artist's Way*, Julia Cameron describes "morning pages," a practice that has become really popular in recent years. The premise is simple: first thing in the morning, fill three pages with longhand, stream-of-consciousness journaling, and *don't* pause writing! It's interesting to see what you can find if you give yourself the time and space to truly comb through all of the thoughts and ideas that have been tucked away in your mind.

Journaling Apps

There are many journaling apps that offer a digital and convenient alternative to writing in a paper notebook. These are great if you're concerned with privacy or keeping your memories safe. A password-protected journal can be carried anywhere that you bring your phone, and your entries will remain safely backed up even if your device goes missing. Some people prefer digital journaling because they can type their entries faster and add multimedia content like photos, videos, and voice clips.

Lately, I've replaced my evening journaling in a paper notebook with the Day One app. I've created a template that automatically populates the entry with headings and numbered lists. I jot down a few sentences about what I did that day, fill out the three things I was grateful for and three wins, and attach a photo I took that day. Easy-peasy!

KEERTHI uses Notion for journaling. She tags each entry with labels for categories like career, personal (goals, relationships), art inspiration, and travel.

Journaling Prompts

You can create a journaling jar by putting prompts on little slips of paper into a jar. Whenever you need some inspiration or a push to think outside the box, pick one and start writing! I also like to keep a note on my Notes app where I'll write down any topics that come to mind that I want to journal more deeply about when I have more time. You can download some of my journaling prompts from the resources page.

Chapter 16

Building (and Breaking) Habits

It takes twenty-one, thirty, or sixty-six days to form a habit, depending on whom you ask. There's really no answer to that question, and habit formation depends on infinite variables. We can set ourselves up for success, though, by designing habits that are easy to stick to and quickly become automatic.

One of the most common mistakes with designing routines and building good habits is that people will find an article of "15 habits to supercharge your health and productivity," resolve to start them all on January 1st, and then get completely overwhelmed, fizzling out long before they've hit day sixty-six or even day ten.

A much better and more sustainable approach is to start small. Pick just one small habit and get it down pat before you even think about adding new ones. Succeeding at a much more manageable goal will give you the motivation to tack on future habits and lead to long-lasting results.

> "Success is the product of daily habits—not once-in-a-lifetime transformations."
> —JAMES CLEAR, *ATOMIC HABITS*

Habit Stacking

Each habit that you develop is a launching pad for new ones. Habit stacking is the practice of tying new habits to already existing ones. Here's an example: let's say you want to start meditating, but you want to start small for now, so your goal is to do two minutes of quiet, focused breathing per day. If you just add that to your to-do list, it'll get pushed further and further down the list of priorities until it's time for bed and you're too tired to even shut your eyes without falling asleep.

To implement habit stacking, pick something that you already do automatically every single day. It doesn't even have to be a habit that you intentionally cultivated. Perhaps you start the coffee machine when you come downstairs every morning. Instead of hanging around, waiting for the coffee mug to fill, set a timer, sit down nearby, and start your focused breathing. Your morning coffee becomes the trigger to your new meditation habit.

❖ *If you want to incorporate more movement into your day...* Trigger: brushing teeth. New habit: doing some squats while you brush.

❖ *If you want to reach your daily step goal...* Trigger: going into work. New habit: taking the stairs instead of the elevator.

❖ *If you want to drink more water...* Trigger: taking Pomodoro breaks. New habit: take a sip of water each time you pause working.

KIMBERLY has done monthly challenges to work on specific habits like not using social media, drinking more water, going outside more often, or writing in a gratitude journal. "Working on just one thing helps you to stay focused," she says, and by isolating one habit at a time to work on, you can better experience the benefits that you gain from it!

Removing Friction

This isn't physics class. For our purposes, "friction" can be defined as any obstacle to completing your habit, like rummaging through your closet for a sports bra or forgetting to bring your water bottle to a two-hour class. Building good habits is not about mustering a superhuman amount of willpower but rather making things as easy as possible. Here are a few ways to "hack" habits:

Outsource reminders. Filling your environment with written reminders like Post-it notes and scheduling timely notifications on your phone are convenient ways to gently nudge yourself throughout the day to get those habits done. One of my daily habits is to go outside for some fresh air and sunshine, so I set up two reminders: one for 12:00 p.m. so that I can consider taking a lunchtime stroll, and one for 3:30 p.m. to see if I can make time to go outside for a few minutes before it gets dark.

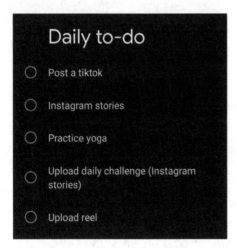

Daily to-do

○ Post a tiktok

○ Instagram stories

○ Practice yoga

○ Upload daily challenge (Instagram stories)

○ Upload reel

Antonia, a student in creative business from Bulgaria, keeps her daily tasks front and center on her phone. Every time she checks it, she's reminded of what she needs to do each day: post on her various social media platforms and practice yoga.

Prepare. When you wake up early in the morning to go for a run or come home from a stressful day to make a healthy dinner, how nice would it be if your running shoes and clothes were all laid out for you, or if the veggies were already all chopped up in the fridge? Try to think of ways that you can smooth the road to checking off the habit. It can be as simple as filling up your water bottle before you go to bed so that you can drink from it as soon as you wake up.

Choose the fun way. There's a mental trap we fall into by thinking that healthy and productive habits necessarily *have* to be difficult and boring... why? If you don't like running, and your end goal is simply to incorporate more movement into your day, why not try a group exercise class or swimming? If you want to practice mindfulness but can't stand sitting still, why not listen to a walking meditation?

Set a date. Putting something on the calendar as a non-negotiable commitment forces you to follow through. Rather than hemming and hawing at home about whether you should pull out your yoga mat for some stretching, you can schedule a yoga class at a studio or simply meet up with a friend in the park to do a yoga video.

Overcoming Bad Habits and Building Good Ones

Almost any action, done repeatedly, that gives your brain some sort of reward, can become automatic. We can harness this property to establish new, positive habits, but what about those old, not-so-great patterns that we get stuck in? These might include going to bed late, checking your email impulsively, or sitting for long periods of time.

We covered how to remove friction to make good habits easier to achieve, but you can pull an Uno reverse card and *add friction to make bad habits more difficult to fall back on.* Let's say you check your email all day long, and that stresses you out in an unproductive way. Instead of relying on sheer willpower to stop opening your inbox, you can use a website blocker to block your email at certain times of the day. If you are spending hours per day scrolling through social media or watching Netflix, delete those apps altogether or deactivate your accounts.

After that, try to *replace the old habit with a better one to distract yourself.* If you delete your social media apps because you've been staying up late scrolling through your phone in bed, you'll suddenly find yourself turning to the TV because you're bored and have time to kill. Try picking up a book instead—it'll still be entertaining, but it won't keep you awake the way the blue light from your screens does, and you might even form a new nightly routine. If you start taking breaks to counteract the time you spend sitting at your desk studying, make a playlist of songs that you can dance to so that you actually look forward to stretching your legs and don't skip out.

Physical habits:
- Taking vitamins
- Skincare
- Exercise

Mental habits:
- Meditation
- Going outside
- Talking to a friend
- Journaling
- Therapy

Productivity habits:
- Updating your budget
- Getting to inbox zero
- Organizing your files
- Tidying your desk
- Cleaning your home

Pick the habits you would like to incorporate into your life and write the "why" behind each. How will this habit benefit your life?

Tracking Your Habits

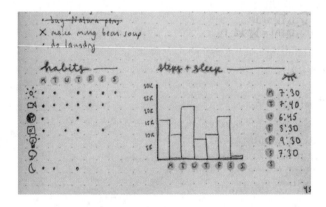

If you prefer an analog method of tracking habits, you can use a sheet of paper to list your habits and mark the days on which you completed them. If you use a bullet journal, you can just dedicate a page each week or month to habits.

Personally, I prefer a digital method so that I can tick off completed habits in the moment. My phone, for better or for worse, is usually nearby, so I can immediately track a finished bottle of water rather than having to go find my notebook. Habit tracking apps can also send automatic reminders and keep track of your streaks. I've used two apps—the Productive Habits app and the Done habits app—and recommend both!

As you track your habits, you might "downgrade" some of your daily habits to a more lenient schedule like "four times per week." For example, my "inbox zero" habit (reaching zero unread emails and messages) is something I would love to do every single day. However, it's usually not realistic. Chances are, on any given day, getting my big projects done is *more* important than responding to every single email, so if I don't get to that magic zero by the end of the day, I don't want to break my habit streak entirely. However, cleaning out my inbox *regularly* is really effective at keeping the flood of incoming communications at bay. Therefore, four times per week strikes a nice compromise between consistency and flexibility.

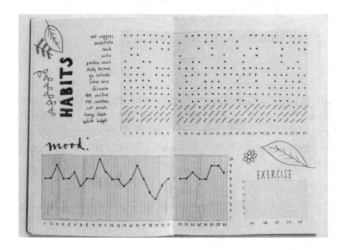

This design is inspired by the spread that Ana uses in her bullet journal to track habits, mood, and exercise.

Reset Routine

We all need a little reset sometimes. Falling behind on your schedule or your habits has a sneaky way of snowballing. Sometimes, it starts because of a really busy week in which one project takes over all of your time and energy. Other times, it's triggered by a slump in motivation. Suddenly, there's clutter scattered around the house, unanswered emails clogging up your inbox, and you could really use a shower.

A reset routine is a great way to press the metaphorical pause button and get yourself back up to speed on everything and give all areas of your life a little boost. Your routine should cover three important categories to your overall wellbeing:

- *Admin*: Get yourself re-aligned with your goals, catch up on your to-do list, and feel on top of things again.
- *Self-care*: Nourish your body and soul with simple activities that were likely pushed to the back burner during a crazy period.
- *Physical*: Set your space in order so that it's clean, tidy, and a joy to be in.

Here are some ideas for your own reset routine:

Admin:

- Answer your emails and messages and get to inbox zero
- Cross of those lingering to-dos that you keep putting off
- Create a plan for the week ahead, so that you can stay on track
- Review your long-term goals, which can fall out of sight during a busy week

Self-care:

- Cook a healthy meal and prep some food to eat in the next few days
- Take a long shower—moisturize, condition, exfoliate, the works!
- Do a fun workout to get your blood flowing
- Spend some time journaling what's on your mind
- Listen to energizing music while you do other tasks
- Schedule some time with loved ones or send someone a text

Physical:

- Declutter an area that has been bothering you
- Tidy up your workspace
- Wash the dishes
- Do the laundry
- Water your plants
- Sweep the floors

What are the steps you can take when you need a physical and mental refresh? Make an "emergency plan" of sorts and write it down somewhere so that when you need it, you'll know exactly what you need to do.

Chapter 17

Mindful Routines

Morning Routine

I'm sure you've seen plenty of videos and articles online that promise a magical morning routine that will make you 200 percent more productive, super rich, and incredibly successful (whatever that means). All you have to do is wake up before the sun is out and follow the "4 a.m. morning routine of the world's most successful billionaires." *Cue infomercial music*

I won't claim that a morning routine will make you a billionaire or even a millionaire, and I don't think you need to wake up at the crack of dawn. I do think, however, that almost anyone can benefit from a simple *morning routine*—a set of habits you group together to get you ready for a successful day.

If you're skeptical, I totally understand why. Morning routines require valuable time that could otherwise be spent sleeping in your warm and cozy bed—it's a costly trade-off! Allow me, someone who absolutely loves sleep but has been practicing a morning routine and waking up early for years, to list my reasons for doing so.

A morning routine sets you up for productivity. Reviewing your goals and your tasks for the day is like having a little morning meeting with yourself. You can make any adjustments that are necessary, think over potential hiccups you'll face, and prioritize in case something urgent comes up and you can't do everything on your to do list.

A morning routine helps you get through that groggy period. Even if you get plenty of sleep, you'll experience a little thing called sleep inertia. It's the period of time after waking that you're still halfway in dreamland. A morning routine that includes a bit of movement, cold water, or caffeine will energize and give you some buffer time before you're expected to be "on" and focused.

A morning routine quiets your mind to focus. Ever wake up with a barrage of thoughts running through your mind already? Taking some time to journal or meditate can quiet the chatter and ensure that your mind won't be cluttered when it's time to focus and get productive!

A morning routine is an act of self-love. Remember how I said that *you* are your most important asset? Before you go out into the world to be your amazing self and make the world a better place, your morning routine is a time to prioritize and check in with yourself to make sure that you've filled your cup.

Basically, if you roll out of bed, throw on some clothes, and rush to grab a banana to eat on the train to work, you're not giving your mind and body the space it needs to prepare for the day. You'll likely be groggier, more scattered, and less centered as you go about your day. If, however, you wake up maybe thirty minutes earlier, do a bit of stretching, take a cold shower, review your plans for the day, and make a healthy breakfast, you'll find that preparation pays dividends over the course of the day. You'll be more alert, focused, and set off a chain of good choices and healthy habits.

Based on the four reasons why you should have a morning routine, there are four categories of morning routine elements that you can choose from to design your own. Keep it simple in the beginning and start with just one simple and easy step in each category.

- *Productivity*: Review your game plan to make sure you have a day free of fumbles. (I believe that's a football metaphor, but to be honest, I don't know much about sports.)
  - ◇ Look over your plan and to-dos for the day
  - ◇ Set three priorities for the day
  - ◇ Choose your one most important task
  - ◇ Check in with your accountability buddy
  - ◇ Review your big goals
  - ◇ Get ready for the day
  - ◇ Pack your bags

- *Energy*: Whether by means of cold water or caffeine, get yourself out of sleepy mode and into "let's get things DONE" mode.
  - ◇ Wake up without hitting snooze
  - ◇ Make your bed
  - ◇ Open the curtains for some sunlight
  - ◇ Crack the window for fresh air
  - ◇ Exercise
  - ◇ Stretch
  - ◇ Take a cold shower
  - ◇ Go on a walk
  - ◇ Have a caffeinated drink

- *Self-care*: It's never too early in the day to treat yourself.
  - ◇ Brush your teeth
  - ◇ Complete your skincare routine
  - ◇ Drink a glass of water
  - ◇ Eat a healthy breakfast
  - ◇ Listen to your favorite playlist
  - ◇ Play with your pet
  - ◇ Listen to a podcast
  - ◇ Read a book

- *Focus*: Quiet all the morning chatter in your mind so that you can focus on what's important.
  - ◇ Journal
  - ◇ Meditate
  - ◇ Take deep breaths
  - ◇ Practice gratitude
  - ◇ Repeat your affirmations

In the morning, **ALICE** likes to step outside with a cup of tea, even if the temperature is freezing. "The fresh air really helps your mental health and makes you feel ready for the day."

As you design your routine, focus on creating something that you can repeat exactly every morning. Once it becomes a habit, you'll never have to wonder, "Hm, what should I do next?" You'll just move automatically to the next step of your routine. This is important because we all have a limited amount of decision-making power that we can use throughout the day! If you save it up in the morning, you'll be able to make better choices throughout the rest of that day.

If you're someone who loves spontaneity and is hesitant to commit to something so structured, remember that consistency *allows* for spontaneity. Starting the day with a consistent routine and a solid plan means you'll be more flexible when any fun opportunities do arise. You'll be able to comfortably adjust your plan, knowing you'll still have time to finish everything you need to get done!

MARIAH has cemented a basic routine of washing her face, eating breakfast, getting dressed, and checking email because she finds that any bit of variability can confuse the body. Once you've established a routine, it can become practically automatic!

SHRUTI swears by her morning routine:

- Wake up
- Stretch for a couple of minutes
- Have water or lemon water
- Wash face
- Brush teeth
- Meditate
- Three-minute breathing exercise
- Check bullet journal, Notion, and Google Calendar
- Read for thirty minutes

Pick and choose your favorite elements to build your own morning routine. Start with just a few steps to keep it simple, then add on others as you get used to your new routine.

Evening Routine

I don't know about you, but I'm always more tempted to skip my evening routine. It just seems so easy to plop right into my cozy bed at the end of a long day. However, I notice that when I skip my evening routine, I feel a bit anxious in the morning. You would think that a good night's sleep would be a complete reset, but somehow, I can still feel the residue of a frazzled evening even after a few sleep cycles.

An evening routine is a chance to take care of your body. At the end of a long day, you might feel tired, sore, and in need of a warm shower, stat. Taking some time in the evening to tend to all of these self-care tasks ensures you'll feel your best when you wake up the next day.

An evening routine is a time to get organized. Isn't it so much nicer to go to sleep when you know that your life and your physical space are in order? Imagine how soundly you'll sleep with tomorrow's to do list already written out, your bags packed, and your bedroom tidied. By practicing these little habits every day, the mess never gets overwhelming.

An evening routine is an invitation to unwind. Going from work straight to bed is not good for your mental nor your physical health, and your quality of sleep will suffer if you don't take some time to relax in between. You might set a firm deadline for when you officially put away the work, sign out of your email, and start your relaxing routine.

An evening routine creates the perfect sleeping conditions. There's so much you can do to improve your sleep quality, from adjusting the thermostat to putting away the blue light sources. Creating a consistent bedtime routine ensures you'll enjoy the best sleep possible every night.

Here are four categories you can pull from to design your own routine:

- *Body*: Time to brush, floss, and pamper. I know that *you* know you shouldn't go to bed without removing your makeup!
  - ◇ Brush your teeth
  - ◇ Stretch tight muscles
  - ◇ Take care of your hair
  - ◇ Moisturize
  - ◇ Remove makeup
  - ◇ Wash your face
  - ◇ Take a warm bath or shower

- *Organization*: Your future morning self will thank you for getting organized and tidying up in advance.
  - ◇ Review your planner
  - ◇ Write tomorrow's to-do list
  - ◇ Review your goals
  - ◇ Take care of a few chores
  - ◇ Pick up your bedroom floor
  - ◇ Pack your bag for tomorrow
  - ◇ Set out your outfit

- *Relaxation*: Shift gradually from your hectic day into quiet sleep mode.
  - ◇ Read
  - ◇ Listen to relaxing music or bedtime stories
  - ◇ Have a warm drink
  - ◇ Meditate
  - ◇ Journal
  - ◇ Practice gratitude
  - ◇ Repeat your affirmations
  - ◇ Watch TV (nothing too scary!)

- *Environment*: Create the optimal sleeping conditions. It's not just the quantity of sleep that matters, but the quality, too!
  ◇ Put away electronics
  ◇ Dim the lights
  ◇ Lower the thermostat
  ◇ Use a noise machine
  ◇ Use essential oils
  ◇ Close the blinds
  ◇ Change into light, comfy PJs

For days when you're simply exhausted and you'd much rather jump straight into bed than crack open a notebook to write about your day, come up with a simplified version of your routine. For example, if I'm really not feeling like doing my entire routine, I just brush my teeth and wash my face. By being flexible, I can maintain some sort of consistent habit rather than skipping my routine altogether and falling off the tracks.

Together, your morning and evening routine form bookends to your day. If you can start and end your day on positive notes, you'll be more resilient to all of the stress and busyness in between. No matter how stressful or difficult your day is, taking some time to practice gratitude and celebrate your wins shines the spotlight of your attention on what went well, improves your mood, and helps you feel more hopeful for the road ahead.

Rainy Days

Occasionally, whether it's because the weather outside is literally gray and drizzly, because your body needs a break, or it's just one of those days, you might wake up to feeling tired and a bit down. You know, as soon as you get out of bed, that you'll have to slog through the day's schedule. While staying in bed and avoiding your responsibilities for the day might not be an option, there are things you can do to work with your energy levels on a rainy day.

First, *don't skip your morning routine.* If you really, really don't feel like doing it, pick and choose the parts of it that energize you. Take a cold shower, stretch, and go outside for a few minutes for some sunshine and fresh air. If you don't see much natural light throughout the remainder of the day, try to take breaks to get outside, or use a light box to achieve a similar effect.

Second, *look at your to-do list for the day and approach it with the mindset of a minimalist.* What's the absolute minimum that you can do today? Some days are more flexible and you might be able to clear a large chunk of your schedule. Other days, it'll be tough to budge a single thing. Try to put off anything that you can and reschedule meetings. If you're afraid you'll upset people, keep in mind that they'd probably prefer to meet with your more energetic, well-rested, and creative self.

At the end of the day, turn to your journal to write, or just think in your head about how the day went. Can you pinpoint a reason why you woke up feeling low today? For example, I've noticed I seem to wake up anxious if I skipped my bedtime routine the night before. With that knowledge, you can make a plan for how you can take better care of yourself. And if you can't find a reason? That's a good lesson, too! We're all just humans, and it's impossible to feel our best *all* the time.

Chapter 18

Tracking (But Not Over-Tracking) Your Life

> "What gets measured gets managed."
> —PETER DRUCKER

You could measure practically everything in your life if you wanted to. But does it all need to be managed? I've definitely fallen into the over-tracking trap before, so I keep asking myself: does the time and energy I invest into tracking this aspect of my life provide some worthwhile insights?

There are areas of life, like my budget, where I want to be really aware of the specifics. I carefully track my income and expenses in a spreadsheet I designed myself. Meanwhile, there are other areas that I don't care about at all, like tracking what I eat. That information is just not relevant to me at this time, and I'd prefer to invest my energy into things that matter more to me! By clarifying what's important to me, I can make progress on my relevant goals without trying to keep tabs on every grain of my life.

Once you pinpoint those goals that might be supported with a bit of data, tracking can really help you to measure your progress and make wise decisions. For example, resources like time and money can be invested most wisely if we are aware of where exactly they are going. So let's talk about how to adopt the mindset of a researcher and start gathering data!

Time Tracking

Time tracking is simply tracking what you do and for how long you do it. At the end of the week, you can see exactly how much time you poured into each bucket of your life. Hmm... fifty hours were spent working. In contrast, you only spent three hours with friends. What can you cut out or complete more efficiently next week in order to move some of those work hours toward meaningful adventures and conversations with friends?

Personally, my favorite benefits of time tracking are not even the bar graphs and pie charts that summarize my results but the awareness that I gain from spending my time in a more intentional way. To quote a cheesy saying, "it's all about the journey, not the destination." People have asked me, *"What do you do with the time-tracking data?"* Honestly, not much. I usually make a note of how many hours I spent on big categories like blogging, health, relaxing, family, and socializing, but I don't go any deeper than that. I let the results guide me in planning my next week, but I don't do any math magic to meticulously shave minutes off one category and add it to another. While you can get that specific if you want to, I encourage you to instead ask yourself questions like, "What is a work task I can delegate next week?" or "What friend can I ask to hang out this week?" By taking these actions, the numbers will start to naturally shift in the direction you want them to.

These are some other benefits that I've experienced from time tracking that are also not very quantitative:

- *I've become more aware of how long certain tasks take.* When I'm blocking out my day, I feel really confident in my estimations of how much time to set aside for each task. I know that writing a newsletter will take me three Pomodoros (three chunks of twenty-five minutes) and that editing and uploading a podcast takes about four hours. Now that I have these accurate estimates, I can set mini-goals for myself and push myself to get things done in an efficient manner.

- *I've limited multitasking and become more focused.* Since you're usually limited to tracking one activity at a time, you have to be really intentional about what you'll spend each chunk of time on. If I'm tracking time spent writing, for example, I can't pop over to another tab to answer emails, because that would be a different activity! As a result, I'm calmer and more focused on the task at hand, and therefore spend *less time* on each individual task.

- *I have to be honest about how I spend my time.* It's incredible how much our brains can distort our sense of time. Time flies when you're having fun and crawls to a standstill when you're waiting at the DMV, but your time-tracking app will always remain honest.

As always, there are a few methods that you can choose from for tracking your time.

You could set up a notebook or a spreadsheet with fifteen- to thirty-minute intervals along the left-hand column and one column for each day of the week. Then, set a reminder on your phone to pause regularly to write down what you did in the last few intervals. This manual method is a bit tedious, but it works just fine for short-term time-tracking experiments.

Otherwise, if you prefer using an app or if you plan on time tracking for any longer than a week or so, there are some great tools out there that will automate the process for you. It takes a bit more setup initially to create and name your tasks, but once that's done, it's just a matter of hitting "start" each time you start a new activity! All of your data will be automatically totaled and displayed in charts, and you can even create sub-tasks, tags, goals, etc., if you want to get that specific. Two apps that I've used and recommend are Now Then Pro and Atracker.

I definitely got way too excited about creating sub-tasks and sub-sub-tasks when I first started time tracking, and I ended up with a lot of data that I really didn't need. Once I realized that, I cut out the clutter and consolidated tasks into bigger umbrella categories. A friend of mine also wanted to try time tracking, but he designed a really simplified version for himself. He created three time-tracking categories: work, relationships, and self, and his goal was to balance those out.

A bit of detail does come in handy sometimes. If you're a graphic designer who works with different clients, for example, you might want to track how much time you spend on each project. If you want to be mindful of how much TV you watch, you might track "reading" and "TV time" as separate tasks instead of lumping them into one task named "relaxing."

However you set up your own personal time-tracking system, keep in mind that it'll take some time to form a habit. Don't get discouraged if you totally forget to track something. You can go back and edit the data, but don't beat yourself up about it if you can't remember what you missed. If you're looking to track your time for a few weeks or more, developing the habit of tracking is more important than the accuracy of the data for now. Eventually, it will become so automatic that you won't even have to think about it.

Track how you spend your time for a week. What surprised you? What changes need to be made to move time between the different "buckets" of your life? On the resources page, I have a master list of time-tracking categories that you can use to pick and choose the activities you'd like to track in your own system.

Budgeting

Let's talk about budgeting!

If you prefer tracking on paper, you can set up a notebook or a page of your bullet journal to track your spending and your income. Of course, all of the usual pros and cons apply here. It's more tangible, so it might make you feel the weight of spending the same way that using cash over a credit card does. However, if you lose it, that's a lot of important information that you can't get back unless you took a photo of it. Plus, doing all of the totaling with a calculator is much more difficult than letting some software do the magic for you. You won't know how much you have left over for groceries unless you flip through all of your transactions and punch your grocery costs into a calculator.

Why should you even bother to track your spending and have a budget? Again, our brains are sneaky little things and fantastic at deceiving us. Just as you might underestimate how long your Netflix binge was because it was *fun*, you're likely to underestimate how much you spent on eating out in the last month because it's *fun*!

Having a budget helps you to reach long-term savings goals. Whether it's for an emergency safety net or a big adventure abroad, having a savings target without a budget is like having a goal without a plan. By keeping an eye on your money and thinking carefully about how much to spend where, you can ensure that a set amount (however small), goes into your savings account each month. EveryDollar has recommendations on their website for what percentage of your budget you should allocate to each category of spending—experiment and find what works for you.

Tracking your spending helps you make better decisions with each purchase. I love this quote from the You Need a Budget website: "You won't be spending less, you'll be spending right." You don't necessarily have to cut out anything and everything that's fun, but you'll become more aware of which purchases are actually adding value and enjoyment to your life and which purchases are just impulse buys that don't live up to their expectations.

You'll notice hidden spending. With the bajillion different TV streaming services out there right now, it's easy to forget you are still paying for one you haven't watched in months. Unless you keep an eye on all of your transactions, those automatic monthly payments can slip past the radar. Wouldn't you rather spend your money on something that you actually use and enjoy?

You'll become more aware of your money overall. Just as with time tracking, it's not just the final tally of your monthly budget that's important, but the actual process of *tracking*. Getting into the habit of writing down or just keeping an eye on where exactly your money is coming from and going to makes you more aware of how you are using this resource. Try to do this every day while the transaction is still fresh in your memory.

There are lots of personal finance apps out there that offer all the money management features you can dream of (if you dream about budgeting, that is). A lot of apps can sync with your bank accounts to automatically pull your transactions so that you don't need to enter them manually. They include lots of tools for estimating your expenses, setting savings goals, viewing charts and reports, etc.

If you don't need or want all of those features, a simple spreadsheet might do the trick! In the past, I have found those personal finance apps a bit too complex for my purposes. I also didn't want the tracking process to be automated; I wanted to manually enter all of my income and expenses so that I would have greater awareness of where my money was going.

As you develop this awareness of your spending, you might develop some strategies for avoiding impulse purchases. KATIE found that she almost never ended up buying what she put into her Amazon "want later" cart. Even if she's thinking, "I want that backpack, that iPad holder, that [fill in the blank] now," soon enough, she'll forget that those things even existed. With online shopping, it's ridiculously easy to just press a button and have something on your doorstep in a day or two. "Let yourself simmer," recommends Katie. "You might stumble upon something at Goodwill that's cheaper and cooler."

On my online resources page, I include an example of my budgeting spreadsheet so that you can see how I set up formulas to tally up all of my transactions across the twelve months of the year and sort them by category. Feel free to make a copy of that spreadsheet and edit it to your heart's content to fit your needs!

Other Things You Can Track

Focus: If you want an incentive to stay focused and off your phone, download an app like Forest. The more time you spend away from your phone, the cuter little animated trees you can grow. The better your focus, the lusher your forest becomes!

Thoughts: A journal is a great way to record thought patterns, or, if you'd like to get quantitative, there are plenty of mood tracking apps out there where you can rate your mood throughout the day and analyze the factors and activities that impact it most.

Fitness: A fitness tracking watch can give you super accurate data on how much you move each day. If you enjoy structured workouts like weightlifting, you can use an app or a notebook to track your exercises and reps, or you can just write down what type of workout you did each day.

Food: You can keep a basic food journal to get a general idea of what categories of food you're eating and how well you're nourishing your body or get into the nitty gritty by logging exactly what you eat into an app with an extensive database of nutritional facts.

Books: Goodreads is a favorite for bookworms to keep track of the books they've read and the millions they still want to read. You can organize books into shelves, set reading goals, and write reviews.

Screen time: Most smartphones have built-in features to show you exactly how much time you're spending on specific apps.

Chapter 19

How to Enjoy
the Process

All this talk of planning, organization, optimization, and *achievement* can get quite overwhelming. Let's pause a bit to talk about how we can actually enjoy the process of working on ourselves and designing our lives without falling into the trap of constant striving.

It's very easy in our modern-day culture to get swept up in the obsession with achievement. Chances are, if you picked up this book, you especially like getting stuff done and achieving the goals that you set for yourself. There's nothing wrong with that! But it's important to keep in mind that you don't *need* that success and achievement in order to be happy.

Laura Thompson, PhD, LPC, believes wholeheartedly that "when we have work that we enjoy and feels meaningful, it can help us feel happier in life." But, she warns, our culture tends to create burnout by constantly pressuring people to do *more*. If we don't clarify our values, we can start to get off balance. "The more our lives align with our values, the greater our sense of peace, happiness, and joy."

Dr. Arlene Weissman developed the Dysfunctional Attitude Scale (DAS), a series of one hundred self-defeating attitudes which are categorized into seven value systems. Self-defeating attitudes in the "achievement" category include "I must be a useful, productive, creative person or life has no purpose" and "If I fail at my work, then I am a failure as a person." In the "perfectionism" category, we've got statements like "If I don't set the highest standards for myself, I am likely to end up a second-rate person." These are harsh, aren't they? We would never tell our friends things like, "If you fail at this project, you're a failure as a person!" Yet, that's the sort of internal dialogue that often runs through our minds.

What would happen if you were to detach yourself from these attitudes? What if there were no prerequisites for your happiness, like, "Oh, I'll be happy once I achieve this goal, or once I'm perfectly organized, or once I earn X amount of money"? I'm not saying that there's no value in setting goals, creating helpful habits, or trying to improve yourself—you can create a more fulfilling, intentional life that way! But what if you enjoyed *the process of getting there*? Your brain is constantly adapting to new levels of success, so chances are that milestone or benchmark you think will be the starting point of your future happiness will lose its luster very quickly, and you'll be back to square one, pinning your happiness to an even bigger, loftier goal and trapping yourself in a constant struggle.

Simply ticking off achievements won't necessarily make you happy in the long run, so accept where you are now and focus on designing a daily life you actually love.

Here are a few more ways to enjoy the process and not just the end result:

Romanticize Your Life

You know when you were little and you'd be in the backseat of the car, driving at night with your head up against the window, listening to the radio and gazing wistfully at the scenery, pretending that your life was a movie? No? Just me? OK, well, my point still stands. There's magic in pretending that you're the main character of a book or a movie. Play some music and dance around while washing the dishes. Pay attention to the colors of the sky when you drive home from work each evening. Bake some chocolate chip cookies and package some up for your friends. Make a tradition out of wearing your favorite autumn sweater when the leaves start to turn colors. Even the most mundane parts of life can appear brighter if you bring some awareness and intentionality to them.

Set Fun Goals

Not all of your goals have to be work-related! Back at the start of the book, we talked about different areas of life and how you envision each to look in your ideal life. Oftentimes, goals are set in the career, health, or finances categories, but to maintain a good balance, show a little love to other categories, like environment, adventures, and relationships! You might set a goal, for example, to redecorate your living room, plan a weekend trip, or to meet up with a friend for lunch every week. Similarly, not all of your routines and habits have to be purely "productive" and practical, either. How about designing a cozy fall evening routine when the weather starts to get chilly (think hot cocoa, books, and pumpkin spiced candles), or making a habit out of listening to holiday music in the winter?

Celebrate Achieving Your Goals

If you expect yourself to hop from one goal to the next with no pauses in between, you'll quickly be reminded of the fact that you're a human being with limited energy who needs rest. Rather than crossing off one project and jumping right into the next, take a moment to feel proud of yourself! You might tell your loved ones so that they can celebrate alongside you, but remember that you don't need anyone else's "permission" to celebrate. So if you've just finished up a tough week of final exams, for example, don't wait until you've received your scores or until your friends are free to celebrate with you to give yourself the space to catch up on any sleep you missed and afford yourself some TLC. You deserve it!

Pay Attention to the Tiny Wins

Some days we are on top of the world, kicking butt and crushing goals, and other days, we just want to stay in bed because *life* is kicking our butts. Every day, but on those difficult ones most of all, it's important to take note of any little accomplishment you can pat yourself on the back for. At the end of each day, I write down three wins. Sometimes I have huge wins to boast about to my journal. "I edited an entire video in one sitting, boo-yah!" Other days it's more like, "I took a shower today and washed my hair" or "I went to bed rather than staying up super late watching TV." Those are huge as well!

Document Your Life

With all this cheesy talk of "the journey is more important than the destination," I think it's important to give some thought to the question of how we can actually document and remember that journey. I recently found some old journal entries where I pondered starting a YouTube channel or complained about staying up late editing videos. These are more meaningful to me than even a YouTube play button, awarded for reaching a subscriber milestone! The award signifies a destination I reached, but the entries reveal the difficult but fulfilling work it took to get there.

When I look back through old photos and videos, there are always plenty of memories captured from family trips and graduations and whatnot, but some of the most special snapshots and clips to look back on are the ones that show a slice of daily life! I like to use the Day One app to jot down a few sentences about what I did each day along with a photo so that in the future, I can look back and see how my daily lifestyle has changed.

PART VI

TROUBLESHOOTING COMMON PRODUCTIVITY PAIN POINTS

Struggling to Find Motivation

No one, I repeat, *no one*, is motivated 100 percent of the time. I can assure you that even the most productive people you know (even the YouTubers you turn to for motivation!) have days when they would very much like to just do *nothing*.

A common misconception is that motivation is something you need to "find," as if it's simply hiding behind your bookcase and if you putter around your room long enough, you'll come upon it and suddenly feel inspired. The flawed logic at the heart of this is the belief that:

Motivation → Action

If you wait for a motivated feeling to strike, it might never arrive. In his book *Feeling Good*, psychiatrist David Burns explains that action *precedes* motivation. It's by starting that dreaded task that we build up momentum, increase our motivation, and thus get into a productive cycle where our tasks start to feel totally doable.

Action → Motivation → More action → More motivation...

One of **ANTONIA**'s non-negotiable daily habits is to read every day. It can be no more than one page, but it *must* be done every day. Oftentimes, when we commit ourselves to a small task, though, we find the motivation to keep going and one page turns into a chapter, which turns into a whole book!

I know exactly what it feels like to put something off for days, weeks... months? It's an anxious feeling in your body. Starting the task feels like the most insurmountable thing in the world. But haven't you done difficult things in the past? Remind yourself of all the times you've successfully faced the beast of procrastination and come out victorious. Visualize yourself in the future—how amazing will it be to cross that task off your to-do list?

Trying to tackle the entire project all at once will probably feel too overwhelming, so write out the tiniest steps that you can start with and set a timer to work for as little as one minute, then pause and make note of how it feels to be making progress. Give yourself a pat on the back! *You are freaking awesome.*

> **MARIAH** has a checklist she turns to when she's feeling unmotivated. It asks: Have you had water? Have you eaten? Have you slept well? Beneath the lack of motivation, you might just be a human being who needs some rest and refueling to function again!

Burns also writes in his book that it can be helpful to write out your irrational thoughts so that you can really see how you've blown the task out of proportion.

Irrational: *I need to get this whole video done today.*
Rational: Do I really need to? Or is it OK to just get a good start on it? Can I ask for a deadline extension?

Irrational: *This is going to be so difficult and impossible.*
Rational: Impossible? You've edited countless videos before! You got all of them done, and some were even easy to edit. There's nothing about video editing that is so terribly difficult or new to you.

Irrational: *I would rather just watch TV for now; this is much more fun.*
Rational: Fun... for now. Keep in mind how stressed out and guilty you feel when you put something off until the last minute! Getting started on the work now will be so much better for your overall wellbeing. I guarantee you'll be happier by the end of the day if you choose to go edit now instead of rewatching all of Queer Eye.

KEERTHI, a future computer science student from India, dreads studying physics even though it's an important subject for her major. When she needs to motivate herself to finish her physics assignments, she'll remind herself of all of the incredible real-world applications of this branch of science, how it can be used to progress toward the goals of the human race, and how it appears in science fiction movies.

If you find yourself constantly unmotivated, or if taking action never seems to work, don't hesitate to reach out to a mental health professional. Things like depression and anxiety can make it difficult to get things done; don't beat yourself up for not simply having the willpower to overcome such an obstacle.

Similarly, if you're *never* motivated to work on the specific goals you've written, it might be time to revisit your big, long-term goals. Did you set them for yourself or for other people? Are they truly aligned with what *you* want to do? If you're not motivated to keep up with your habits, did you truly pick and choose them for yourself or because you saw them in a YouTube video?

KIMBERLY reminds herself daily of why she set her goal in the first place. When her goal was to participate more in class, it was not for her teacher nor for her parents, but for herself—to push herself out of her comfort zone.

SANDRA likes to balance schoolwork with creative work. If she's overwhelmed by the amount of homework she needs to complete and knows she won't have any time left over to be creative, she starts to procrastinate, making the situation even worse! Instead, she tries to plan something to look forward to after getting work done. If she finishes an assignment, for example, she might allow herself to work on editing a video or read a few chapters of a book.

Maintaining an Internal Locus of Control

Keep in mind that, to get the motivation snowball rolling, you don't even have to take action on the thing you're procrastinating. If you're having trouble getting yourself off the couch to go be productive, you might want to start with something that feels easier, like washing the dishes or baking a loaf of banana bread, before you work your way up to bigger actions. It doesn't matter much *what* you do, as long as you do *something* that gives you a sense of control and independence. Look at you, you went and found a recipe for banana bread, got the ingredients, measured and stirred like a boss, and created something delicious entirely of your own volition!

Cultivating this belief that your actions have an impact on your life and your surroundings is also known by the term "internal locus of control," coined by American psychologist Julian Rotter. Having an internal locus of control means that you believe your decisions decide your outcomes, while having an external locus of control means you believe your destiny is controlled by luck, fate, and other sources outside of you.

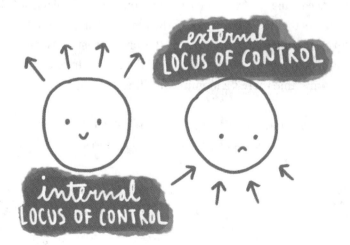

Is one any better than the other? Absolutely! Research suggests that people with an internal locus of control are more successful in work and academics, have lower stress levels, and tend to live longer. On the other hand, people who believe that their circumstances are totally out of their control experience learned helplessness and depression. In a 1976 study, Langer and Rodin[1] found that nursing home residents who had even one opportunity to exercise choice experienced increased mood, quality of life, and longevity. A 2011 article titled "Born to Choose"[2] states that healthy individuals actually overestimate how much personal control they have over situations that are totally up to chance, like the lottery! So maybe don't go out and buy several hundred lottery tickets, but do have the confidence of someone who believes that they *could* win the lottery out of sheer force of will.

Procrastination

There's an amazing TED Talk by Tim Urban called "Inside the Mind of a Master Procrastinator" that my AP English Language teacher made our class watch when we were all procrastinating on a writing project. According to Urban, procrastination is a result of a whole host of characters that live in your mind: the Instant Gratification Monkey who loves all things easy and fun, the Rational Decision-Maker, who actually gets important things done, and the Panic Monster, who wakes up anytime there's a looming deadline or crisis.

The talk is entertaining and amusing at first—isn't that a great representation of what goes on when we imagine a sleep-deprived

---

1 Ellen J. Langer and Judith Rodin, "The Effects of Choice and Enhanced Personal Responsibility for the Aged: A field Experiment in an Institutional Setting," *Journal of Personality and Social Psychology* 34, no. 2 (1976): 191–198, https://doi.org/10.1037//0022-3514.34.2.191.

2 Lauren A. Leotti, Sheena S. Iyengar, and Kevin N. Ochsner, "Born to Choose: The Origins and Value of the Need for Control," *Trends in Cognitive Sciences* 14, no. 10 (2010): 457–463, https://doi.org/10.1016/j.tics.2010.08.001.

student drinking cups of coffee in order to crank out, in one night, an entire project they had four weeks to do? Near the end, it takes on a more somber tone, however. What about that book you want to write, the business you want to start, or the painting hobby you keep telling people you're planning to start? When is the Panic Monster going to get things moving if there is no deadline?

At the end, Urban showed what he called a "Life Calendar." Each week of a ninety-year life was represented by a tiny little square. It was sobering. How could that possibly be it? I thought about how quickly a week flies by... Monday, Sunday, Monday, Sunday, and each of those weeks ticks off yet another box.

Take a look at the first section on how to troubleshoot a lack of motivation; those tips will help you out with procrastination. Often, when we're putting something off, we are waiting for some magic feeling of motivation to strike (spoiler: it might never come). Take a little bit of action and get the ball rolling before the Panic Monster wakes up!

Criticizing yourself for procrastination will only lead to a spiral of self-hatred. **KYLA** finds that the more she puts herself down for procrastinating, the more she ends up procrastinating! Show yourself kindness, treat yourself the way you would treat a friend, and move on.

MAWADDA, an electrical engineering student in Sudan, agrees. She tries to be easy on herself when she finds herself procrastinating. "I ask myself: why am I procrastinating? Am I feeling down? Is the task so big that I'm afraid to start?" If it's a mental thing and I'm just feeling down, I'll take a day to relax and take care of myself. If it's fear of the amount of work that I have, I break down the task and do the smallest thing for one Pomodoro and not think about anything else.

When I don't feel like filming a video, I remind myself of my own "why." I am working to create something that inspires people and helps them to live a better, more fulfilling life. With that goal in mind, the dreaded task suddenly becomes more purposeful.

CARLOTTA, a student in Germany, says it's important to "always get started no matter what, even if it's just typing in the name of the website" you'll need for your work. When she is intimidated by a large task, she'll break out her journal to write about what specifically she's afraid of and how she can break it down into less anxiety-inducing steps.

Working with an Unpredictable Schedule

Scheduling out your week in advance is all good and fine as long as your schedule is consistent and random tasks don't keep cropping out of nowhere for you to deal with ASAP. To a certain extent, you should try to pare down your commitments and set boundaries with others to limit this as much as possible. But oftentimes, unpredictability and variability are inevitable! You might work at a job where you don't know what the day's tasks will be until you arrive each day, or maybe you have irregular hours or an on-call schedule.

These are challenging constraints to work within, so before anything, keep in mind that you're not a robot and give yourself grace!

In these cases, it's helpful to look at your schedule and look for any opportunities to add a bit of consistency to your day. Perhaps you can commit to a morning and evening routine that will serve as bookends to your day that you can count on no matter what happens in between.

Maybe you have a lunch break during which you'll take a daily walk to move your body and refresh your mind.

You'll also need to be careful to set realistic goals. If your goal for the week requires that you use absolutely all of the time you have available and doesn't account for a single unexpected project or distraction, you should edit your goal to give yourself a bit of leeway.

Don't discount the planning and organization process, either. It's not an all-or-nothing game! Even if you can't plan completely or follow your plan perfectly, it doesn't mean there was no value in taking the time to plan. By keeping your tasks and priorities organized, you can stay on top of things and simply shuffle and move your work around as situations arise and schedules shift. The water may get choppy, but at least you still have a boat and a paddle to work with!

Sticking to a
Long-Term System

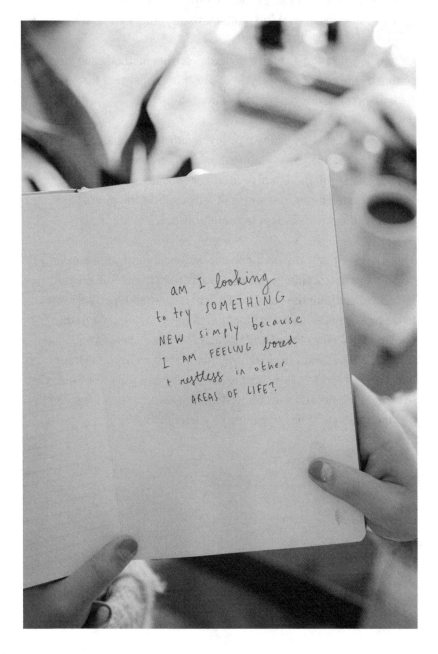

am I looking
to try SOMETHING
NEW simply because
I AM FEELING bored
+ restless in other
AREAS OF LIFE?

You know when you find a new productivity tool and you get so excited about it you spend the whole day setting it up and tinkering with the features... but by the next month you're sick of it or you've found something even shinier and more tempting to try out?

Or maybe you come up with a new goal-setting method each month, so that by the end of the year, there's nothing consistent for you to review and measure your progress by.

If you're prone to this "shiny new toy" syndrome, pause before you're tempted to change any of your systems. When faced with the option of trying a new method/tool or leaving good enough alone, I always lean toward the latter. Is it worth disturbing how things are working currently to learn and adapt to something new?

There are definitely times when your system is simply *not working*, and if there's something you can do to fix that, then by all means, go right ahead! But the question I ask myself when I feel like I want to change something is: *Am I looking to try something new simply because I'm feeling bored and restless in other areas of life?* I often find that when I want to change my planning systems, I'm either looking for a way to procrastinate getting the real work done or trying to combat a general sense of boredom that could be cured instead by picking up a new hobby or calling up a friend!

Consistency is really rewarding. If you find something that works and you stick with it, then not too far into the future, you'll have a shelf of neat bullet journals to flip back through or a tidy record of monthly goals that you can review and evaluate. Let that motivate you to stick with your system and keep things simple!

Systems That Are Too Complicated

When you're creating a system for planning and organizing, it's easy to go overboard with a complicated task management system and suddenly find yourself drowning in tasks, sub-tasks, and sub-sub-tasks, labels in every color of the rainbow, and eight different levels of priority.

Doesn't that make you anxious? It definitely does not evoke the sort of calm and peaceful feeling that I'm looking to achieve through staying organized!

As fun as all of the extra bells and whistles may seem, really ask yourself if an extra tool, feature, or system will help in the long run. If you think it might, give it a test run for a week or so! Don't be afraid to cut it out whenever it stops being useful. You always want to simplify, simplify, simplify!

You know I love tracking—time, habits, budgets, etc.—but I keep these systems just as detailed as they need to be, no more, no less! In time tracking, I used to have ultra-detailed tasks like recording podcasts, shooting photos, filming videos, editing videos, and editing podcasts. Whew! Maybe I should have gone as far as to track the time I spent managing my time tracking system! After a while, I realized that this information just *wasn't* helpful. At the end of each week, I liked going back to see how much time I spent relaxing, how much time I spent on my blog, etc., but I simply never needed to see exactly how much time I spent on each individual task!

When I plan, I try to set a time limit for how much time I'll spend on the process. For weekly planning, that's usually an hour to an hour and a half. Anything longer than that and I know I've probably gotten distracted or am getting bogged down in unimportant details. Setting a time limit keeps you moving and thinking quickly!

Overall, I'm a big believer that less is more. Whether you're trying to manage your to-dos, organize your stuff, or set goals, try to err on the side of *less*. At the end of the day, planning and organization help us to focus on what matters most and achieve a sense of peace. More than that, and your planning routines can actually become a source of stress confusion. Life is just more enjoyable when you go with the flow!

Sometimes you just have to take imperfect action and trust the process.

Mental Wellness and Perfectionism

Through planning and organization, we can aim to design a life that gives us the space to take care of ourselves *and* do the things that we want to do. That is, of course, easier said than done, as the thrilling pursuit of goals can often take precedence over our own wellbeing. We're all prone to comparing ourselves to other people—classmates, coworkers, friends, random strangers on the internet... People can fall into the trap of worshipping at the altar of productivity while overworking themselves to the point of irritability, sleeplessness, anxiety, and depression.

Mental health counselor Laura Thompson views mental health as a continuum. If we don't manage the stressors that life throws at us, it can negatively impact our mental health, and we can turn to ineffective coping strategies. For example, some people abuse substances such as alcohol or other drugs, which can lead to more significant issues. Others throw themselves into their work to avoid dealing with uncomfortable feelings. Thompson believes that it's important that we get to know ourselves and how to best manage the challenges that come our way. By giving ourselves downtime to journal, think, and just be, we slowly become experts of ourselves and can recognize whether we're properly managing our stress.

Gary Robinson, Director of Counseling at Hartwick College and consultant at P3 Mental Health, points to perfectionism as a common cause of mental health struggles. He explains that when we have low self-esteem, "We overcompensate by trying to always stay busy, focusing only on external achievement, and seeking external rewards like high grades. Ask yourself if your excessive focus is to try to artificially inflate your self-worth or if it is internally driven and done for health reasons."

You don't have to adopt every strategy; just pick a few tools that support your life. If you feel anxious, evaluate. Is your schedule too rigid, your goals too unrealistic, or your focus too scattered?

If you're in a place where you are really struggling but don't have much of a choice to step back from your commitments, Thompson recommends, first and foremost, having compassion for yourself. Sometimes things feel like they're just too much. In these moments, self-care is particularly important. It can also be helpful to reach out for support. Call upon your resources for guidance and let go of what isn't absolutely necessary. You might ask a professor, for example, if you can take an incomplete, or turn something in late so that you can take an evening off.

Jealousy and Comparisonitis

A few things to keep in mind:

Everyone has hidden struggles. Every time I've had a deep conversation with someone whose life I had previously assumed to be perfect, successful, and beautiful, I was shocked to learn how much more there was behind the screen (behind the Instagram profile, in many cases). You may envy certain aspects of someone's life, but it's likely that they have things they're struggling with behind the scenes, and they would envy certain aspects of yours.

On a similar note, *your perception is not the reality*. Most of us are pretty great at pretending that we're OK. In certain situations, these acting chops come in handy. Other times, they keep us from honestly relating to the people around us. I'm often surprised at how quickly I can turn it "on" for an event and step into my energetic, positive persona, even if I was feeling sad and lonely beforehand. So if you feel like you're surrounded by people who are all doing fine, chances are, it's just an illusion. Having honest conversations and reminding each other that "it's OK to not be OK" makes all the difference.

Focus on the possibility. This is all about the abundance mindset. I recently went to a dance exercise class where the crowd is always full of cheerful and upbeat people. It was a Friday evening, and everyone was greeting each other, smiling, and getting pumped to start their weekend on an energized note. I happened to be feeling really low that day, and I was surprised at how bitter I suddenly became. I felt like I was separated from everyone else by a screen, watching them enjoy themselves so easily. My internal dialogue was running. "I used to be happy like that, why can't I be happy? It's so annoying how happy they are." But then I realized, I *have* been a part of that crowd before! If I changed my interpretation, then seeing everyone else having a good time served as a reminder of what I would soon experience again once I got through this rough patch!

Michelle Barnes, the creator behind the personal development YouTube channel *MuchelleB*, shared three ways she combats comparisonitis.

1. Rather than thinking "*Why not me?*" when she finds herself comparing her achievements to those of other online creators, she tries to hype them up. Intentionally choosing a supportive attitude over a competitive one shifts your energy from resentment to more of a "we're all in this together" kind of vibe.

2. "Recognize that different people have different resources: energy, money, help, family, etc." You can't directly compare your achievements to anyone else's because we all have a different starting place in the race. "That can make such a big difference when it comes to what people are outputting in the world." The only yardstick you can measure yourself with is your own.

3. Finally, muting posts from people online is an easy way to quiet the chatter for the benefit of your mental health. "You don't need to see everything that everyone is doing on social media."

CAROLINE says that the key to preventing imposter syndrome as a student at a large and competitive US university is to surround yourself with people who don't flaunt their achievements, but rather support others and form communities to prop each other up. "It doesn't matter what the person next to you is doing," she says. "Connect with your advisers to help you meet the goals you want to meet."

SAHAANAA had this to say on the topic of comparisonitis: "I have come to the mindset that everyone is on a different path. Even if we may have the same destination, I cannot compare my chapter to someone else's chapter. They might have encountered some plot twists. Technically, I'm not behind, I'm just getting to the destination in a different way."

Success with Learning Disabilities

Students with learning disabilities like dyslexia (which makes it difficult to read quickly and automatically) often also have trouble with executive functioning skills—*the skills we use to plan and organize our time and resources in order to focus on completing complicated tasks.*

Erin Braselmann is the Associate Director of Student Accessibility Services at Yale. She defines a learning disability as any condition that negatively affects a person's ability to learn. Dyslexia is probably the most commonly known, but there are others like auditory processing disorder as well as dyscalculia (difficulty with math) and dysgraphia (difficulty with writing). To find out if they have an LD, people usually get full neuropsychological evaluations and a full battery of learning assessments that display much lower scores in specific areas.

When we're talking about planning and organizing, we need to remember that the playing field is not level to start with. Students with learning disabilities have to work longer and harder than their peers to succeed in school and beyond, so it's important that they receive the help they need.

"Having accommodations in school is essential," says Erin. "If you are dyslexic and reading takes you three times as long as your peers, no amount of strategies will really make that go away." In that case, audiobooks, text-to-speech software, or having things read aloud are examples of accommodations that allow the student a fair opportunity to demonstrate their intelligence on a reading assignment or exam.

Second, a supportive learning environment makes all the difference in helping students to embrace their disability. "A bunch of people with learning disabilities grow up feeling like there's something wrong with them, like they're not as intelligent," so they have trouble asking for help because they'd prefer people not to know they have an LD in the first place. "We talk in my office about a disability as an identity," says Erin, "We try to reframe it positively." She wants students to know that there's nothing wrong with them and that having an LD is a normal part of the human experience. The fact that Erin works at the Student Accessibility Services department at an elite university like Yale is proof that students with an LD can be incredibly successful!

The Frostig Center, a nonprofit organization for students with LDs, has identified "proactivity" as one of the "success attributes" that helps individuals to succeed with an LD. Erin helps students practice this self-advocacy by modeling conversations with faculty members and she encourages them to form positive relationships with supportive folks in the student accessibility department and anyone else at the school who will advocate for them.

Not all learning disabilities will affect people's ability to plan and organize. In her work, for example, Erin has "seen students with the same diagnosis as another student have executive functioning really impacted, and others not so much." For those students who struggle with juggling their workload, many schools have academic support staff who can help with acquiring the time management and planning skills they need to succeed in school. Students can, for example, work with an academic adviser to figure out how to spread the work of a twenty-page paper over the course of a month. They might make a weekly appointment with a writing tutor to stay on track.

The students Erin works with have also found these strategies helpful:

- *Calendar apps*: A lot of students, especially in the younger generation, deploy technology to manage their homework and schedule. They might use a calendar to block out everything from work and classes to meals and leisure, then set up notifications to remind themselves of what they should be doing at any point in the day.

- *Consistent wake time and bedtime*: Students find that going to sleep and waking up at the same time each day makes it easier for them to stay on track.

- *Find a distraction-free environment*: "We live in a world where our attention is always split." At any moment, a text or a call could interrupt your workflow when you need to get difficult reading or writing done. Find a quiet study room (or an environment with ambient noise) and turn off your phone (including all notifications).

- *Take breaks*: If you focus on one thing for too long, "You get to a point where you're not getting the information that you're supposed to be acquiring and not doing your best work."

Braselmann encourages students to not compare their progress with that of other students, which can be especially challenging at a school like Yale. "When you have a strong sense of who you are, your identity, a good worldview, and a healthy outlook, you would know that some people do certain things at different times and life is not about a timeline."

A study in the pediatrics journal *Children*[3] interviewed fifty-two college students with learning disabilities and/or attention deficit hyperactivity disorder (ADHD) to learn about what strategies helped them to cope with time-related and productivity challenges. These included:

- Waking up early and blocking off the morning hours to get important work done or to catch up on daily tasks like cooking and cleaning before focusing on work and academics.
- Talking to other students with LD/ADHD to compare notes on strategies and get ideas on how to improve their own systems.
- Setting up triggers for working, like opening up a certain computer window the night before writing a paper or placing the laundry hamper where it's easily visible.
- Planning fun activities as motivation to finish work.

---

3 Consuelo M. Kreider, Sharon Medina, and Mackenzi R. Slamka, "Strategies for Coping with Time-Related and Productivity Challenges of Young People with Learning Disabilities and Attention-Deficit/Hyperactivity Disorder," *Children* (Basel, Switzerland) 6, no. 2 (2019): 28, https://doi.org/10.3390/children6020028.

So... What Now?

I truly hope the tips and methods outlined in this book help you to design a simple, organized system that allows you to feel on top of things, achieve your goals, and do so in a happy and calm way. Now that you've gone through every section and filled your brain with planning tools and routines, it's time to bring all of that together and consolidate it into your own personal planning and organization system. We covered:

- Keeping a calendar for appointments and time blocking

- Managing your tasks and projects in a proactive way

- Setting effective long-term goals and following through with regular planning routines

- Organizing a workspace you love

- Note-taking methods for students and anyone else

- Healthy working habits to maximize your time and energy

- Productivity "hacks" (that are really just well-tested and solid techniques)

- Using your digital tools in a mindful way

- Scheduling time for self-care (because you are your most valuable asset)

- Habits to improve your life

- Routines to streamline and simplify your day

- And more

Of course, setting up this system might just be the easy part. It's following through with it that's the tough part. But now that you're armed with all of this knowledge, you're well-equipped to face those challenges. Now you know that if you ever get unmotivated, you need to simply take *one* action to watch your motivation come back. If you ever feel burned out, you'll have healthy and mindful habits to fall back on to reenergize yourself. If you ever get distracted, you'll have a whole range of productivity tricks up your sleeve and an accountability buddy to text.

As you grow and your life changes, your system will have to grow and change as well. The way you managed your homework in college may not work for the job you get after graduating. Moving out on your own may introduce a whole plethora of new responsibilities to manage like finances, cooking, and housekeeping. You might take your system down a notch in terms of complexity if you find yourself feeling overwhelmed. Changing your system to suit your needs is perfectly OK. The foundational habits, like checking in with a "keystone" each day, remain, and I promise you they will make a huge difference in your life when you stick to them.

These habits turn your "somedays" into solid plans, aimless busyness into purposeful work, and your dream life into a reality.

Use this space to summarize the planning system you've developed.

- ◇ My daily routine
- ◇ My daily habits
- ◇ My task management (Where will my tasks live? How often will I check in to plan the next tasks?)
- ◇ My calendar (What calendar tool will I use? How will it be structured?)
- ◇ Productivity and organization techniques I will implement
- ◇ What stuck with me the most from this book?

ACKNOWLEDGMENTS

Thank you to my editor, Jane Kinney-Denning, and the entire team at Mango for helping this first-time author cross something off her bucket list way earlier than she'd expected. This is the longest thing I've ever written, by far (aside from the terrible novel I wrote in seventh grade, which has been rightfully buried in the depths of time), and without you I would not have been able to shape it into the polished book that it is now and share it with such a large audience.

Thank you to my mom and dad for all of the opportunities you've given me in my life, for your daily love, and for letting me post stuff on the internet since middle school. YouTube might not have been around when you were my age, but you saw the potential even when I doubted it. Thanks also (I guess) to my brother, for making fun of my YouTube channel once in a while—it kept my ego in check. You're actually really supportive and you make me laugh every day. Love ya.

Thank you to my lovely friends all around the world. I am grateful for your presence in my life every day. I can talk to you about literally anything, and many of my video ideas stem directly from the deep conversations we have.

Thank you to all of my teachers over the years for imparting the academic knowledge you were hired to teach, but more importantly, for the life lessons that I got as a free bonus. You shaped me into the person I am today. Thank you, especially, to Mr. Frontier, for being one of the first people to push me to continue pursuing my YouTube channel. Even though I was embarrassed when you pulled it up on your screen during class and started watching my videos, your encouraging words came at just the right time.

Finally, thank you to all of the readers and viewers of *The Bliss Bean*. Your messages, comments, and emails make me feel so loved. I am constantly inspired by your efforts, and it is a huge honor for me to be any small inspiration in your life. This community is the best.

beatrice ♡

ABOUT BEATRICE

Beatrice Naujalyte is a college student and the creator behind *The Bliss Bean*, a popular YouTube channel with planning and personal development tips for those seeking to design a meaningful and joyful life. Since 2018, the channel has grown to over 200K subscribers and over ten million total views. Beatrice's videos on planning, organization, and self-care, including a video about study tips and memorization techniques that has surpassed one million views, have inspired and motivated her audience to pursue their goals and transform their lives. Now also encompassing a weekly newsletter with over 20K readers and a podcast with thousands of listens, *The Bliss Bean* is a tight-knit community of individuals who are passionate about personal growth.

Mango Publishing, established in 2014, publishes an eclectic list of books by diverse authors—both new and established voices—on topics ranging from business, personal growth, women's empowerment, LGBTQ studies, health, and spirituality to history, popular culture, time management, decluttering, lifestyle, mental wellness, aging, and sustainable living. We were recently named 2019 *and* 2020's #1 fastest-growing independent publisher by *Publishers Weekly*. Our success is driven by our main goal, which is to publish high-quality books that will entertain readers as well as make a positive difference in their lives.

Our readers are our most important resource; we value your input, suggestions, and ideas. We'd love to hear from you—after all, we are publishing books for you!

Please stay in touch with us and follow us at:

Facebook: Mango Publishing
Twitter: @MangoPublishing
Instagram: @MangoPublishing
LinkedIn: Mango Publishing
Pinterest: Mango Publishing
Newsletter: mangopublishinggroup.com/newsletter

Join us on Mango's journey to reinvent publishing, one book at a time.